IAN COURT was born in Southampton, England and was educated at Sussex University and the University of Illinois. He joined Voluntary Service Overseas after the University of Sussex and served in Sierra Leone, West Africa. The VSO experience certainly helped, or perhaps hindered, the shaping of his character, his sense of humor and his somewhat dangerous sense of the ridiculous.

The tropical rain forests of Sierra Leone gave way to the temperate plains of central Illinois and, after three years of study, he was prevailed upon to run a nine-month university project in Puerto Rico. So the Illinois plains gave way to a tropical island in the Caribbean. Thirty-six years later he is still there.

Recruited to work as a lobbyist for the Puerto Rican Government, he spent several years commuting to Washington in the era of Jimmy Carter. The creation of his own consulting company in 1980 continued that work and expanded his horizons to the private sector. He currently works as a process consultant to the pharmaceutical and food industries on the Island and sells commercial boats in the Caribbean; interestingly, the British boat builder he represents is part of a major industrial group, which includes the company his father worked for all his life.

In 1986 came an offer to become Honorary British Consul for Puerto Rico. Ten years later, when trade and investment had increased significantly, he was honored with an OBE for services to Britain. In 2001 the British Government established a full career post in San Juan and Ian retired. In the meantime, he had founded, and continues to run, the Puerto Rico/United Kingdom Chamber of Commerce, a non-profit organization, which has a membership of over a hundred and twenty. The Chamber has become a think-tank for Puerto Rican economic development and provides an independent forum that is unique on the island.

This is his first published book, with subsequent works in various stages of development. His hobbies include restoring classic MG cars, traveling and organizing and running car rallies.

Ian lives in Old San Juan, Puerto Rico.

Funny, Serious, and Just Plain Stupid

FUNNY, SERIOUS, AND JUST PLAIN STUPID

IAN COURT

ATHENA PRESS
LONDON

FUNNY, SERIOUS, AND JUST PLAIN STUPID
Copyright © Ian Court 2007

ISBN 10-digit: 1 84401 797 4
ISBN 13-digit: 978 1 84401 797 3

First Published 2007 by
ATHENA PRESS
Queen's House, 2 Holly Road
Twickenham TW1 4EG
United Kingdom

Printed for Athena Press

TABLE OF CONTENTS

PREFACE

"Put a shot across their bows…"

"My inspired challenge was three laps of the pool—naked!"

"What started as an only child looking for his birth mother ended with uniting three families, a mother and father, seven brothers, and a sister."

"…IRA machine guns, bombs and bazookas—and his battery was flat!"

"The yacht was found by HMS London *six months later after drifting for 2700 miles in the North Atlantic."*

"they…tried to entice two septuagenarians to dance with them."

These are excerpts from some of the stories that make up this book. All the stories are true but, as the table of contents indicates, truth is certainly stranger than fiction. Each story is taken from my fifteen years experience as the Honorary British Consul in San Juan, Puerto Rico.

When I was appointed to the post in San Juan two friends sent me copies of Graham Greene's book *The Honorary Consul*. That book was the only written instruction I ever received. The fact that it was sent by two friends and not by the British government should have warned me but then, as I subsequently learned, bureaucrats do not generally have a sufficient sense of the ridiculous to send such instructions. (*The Honorary Consul* and my book are quite different but the central theme of anachronism runs through both.)

I am grateful to my friends and to Graham Greene for giving me inspiration and for giving me some extremely pertinent quotes.

Graham Greene's book is a delightful tale of a British honorary consul appointed to Uruguay in South America. The author toured the area, in preparation for writing, and his encounters defined some of the characters he used in his plot. Whether any of the people he met were actually honorary consuls is unknown, but the visit enabled him to place his chief character in a local perspective. His book, as an instruction manual for my new position, however, was a little short on relevant information. If I had been kidnapped for ransom, like his main character, it might have been quite useful but, even though my tenure in Puerto Rico was quite exciting at times, I cannot boast being kidnapped. Obviously I was not important enough in anybody's mind to be worth ransoming!

Ironically, an honorary consul in Puerto Rico was kidnapped a few years before I assumed my post, but he was returned unharmed a few days later—not worth ransoming, as I said!

Funny, Serious, and Just Plain Stupid portrays the peculiar status of honorary consuls. They are an anomaly, if not an anachronism. Nobody quite knows what to do with them or how to handle them—least of all their own governments! And, in true bureaucratic fashion, if you cannot understand something, let alone control it, you simply ignore it.

I did once try and decipher the British diplomatic hierarchy with a view to determining where my position actually fell. I finally gave up the struggle. The titles were just too obscure. On reflection, that was probably intentional—heaven forbid that anyone should be able to tell what a bureaucrat was supposed to do just by reading his title. The only conclusion I did reach was that honorary consuls are at the bottom of that hierarchy and therefore positioning myself on the 391st rung of the diplomatic ladder sounded reasonable.

In the bureaucratic mind, lowly positions, by their very nature, do not require any training since they are not thought to require very much work. I obviously fell into that category since I received no training at any point in my illustrious fifteen-year consular career. I can only think that the very act of arriving at the ivory tower of honorary consulship somehow endowed me with all the knowledge and expertise I needed; through some sort of osmosis?

I don't suppose I could really have done all that much damage from such a lowly position but I was representing Her Majesty's government. Letting me loose without instructions did require a certain amount of faith—or perhaps they didn't know what I was supposed to do either. It is vaguely possible that since they didn't pay me they realized they were in no position to tell me what to do, but that's highly unlikely given the normal bureaucratic mindset.

I did give myself some training, however. After an exhaustive search I managed to obtain a copy of Michael Caine's film *Water*. The film chronicles the life of a British consul on a small Caribbean island—the movie was filmed on Saint Lucia in the Grenadines. The film is hilarious in typical Michael Caine style but becomes even more so once you realize that most of the script is pretty close to the truth. I have been subsequently informed by reliable sources that *Water* is required viewing for all British diplomats posted to the Caribbean and for those posted to many other small jurisdictions. I fully recommend the film to anyone with a good sense of humor although I am slightly amazed that the British government has the vision and the audacity to recommend its viewing, albeit unofficially—maybe there's hope yet!

You may well be wondering at this point, what exactly *is* an honorary consul and why would anyone write a book about such an insignificant position.

The position, as the title implies, is honorary in the sense that you receive no salary. It does not necessarily mean that you are automatically honorable, although, of course, we all are! Some countries offer "honorariums"—translation: pittances—to their honorary consuls and some pay operating expenses such as reimbursing the cost of postage stamps and secretarial services but, basically, it is a non-paying position.

Many countries in the world employ honorary consuls. The notable exception among the larger nations is the United States. That anomaly causes many problems when agreements of reciprocal courtesies are involved—how can you offer reciprocity when you don't have anything that is reciprocal? I have asked many people why the U.S. does not participate in this wonderful system but I have yet to receive a sensible reply, let alone an authoritative one.

Countries try to select prominent individuals, who reside in the country in question, to represent their interests for free. It is a marvelous way of having excellent (my bias) representation without it costing the budget a penny. Some countries require their honorary consuls to be their own citizens but many do not. The duration of the appointments can be for a fixed term or, in some cases, it is hereditary. There are many variations but the common denominator is that you work for nothing, at least in a fiscal sense.

A description of the position begs the question of why I feel the need to inflict my experiences on the general reading public. In my defense, I have to say that, despite my fights with the bureaucracy, the experience of honorary consul was one of the most challenging, entertaining, unbelievable, fascinating, and satisfying, non-paying jobs I have ever had in my life. However, my experiences as honorary consul are obviously interesting to me and, perhaps, even to my family. But why should they have greater appeal? My justification is two-fold.

First, in the generic sense, I feel it is a story that deserves to be told. There are countless honorary consuls throughout the world working at least as hard as their paid counterparts, if not harder. In many cases they are more effective because they want to do the job, they know the local scene well and they are not just per-forming for a pay check. That is a little unfair, I realize, but perhaps less unfair than we would like to think. Honorary consuls operate in many different environments. Some are hazardous, some routine, some interesting, but all are demanding. And, at the end, they slip away into oblivion, usually with their country's thanks but sometimes with not even that. (For example, the British government recently discovered they had an honorary consul in one of the French Caribbean Islands. They had totally forgotten about the person for many years!)

Graham Greene's portrait of an honorary consul as a bum-bling drunkard, reinforced by Michael Caine's character in the film *Water* quietly smoking a joint with the local priest, may do justice to some people who have held such positions (no personal comments about this author allowed) but, generally, they do not reflect the excellent work that honorary consuls perform.

The second reason for inflicting my experiences on you is the great encouragement I have received from the many people who have heard the stories that follow. These audiences have been fascinated, amazed, and have generally demanded more. (It's tempting to think that these responses reflect my amazing storytelling abilities, but I doubt it. As someone once told me, "You couldn't make this stuff up if you tried.")

This book is a collection of stories, incidents, and sagas that I encountered in my tenure as Honorary British Consul in San Juan, Puerto Rico from 1986 until my retirement in 2000. One story pre-dates this period, but only by a few months. I have selected the stories from a vast collection covering that fifteen-year period. It has been tempting to tell only the ones that produce strong emotions but, in the interest of balance, I have interlaced the more obviously appealing stories with others of a more serious nature. The choice reflects my own somewhat irreverent perspective and includes many stories that still make me chuckle years later. In some cases I have added commentary, in others not. In most cases the stories are told as they happened without too much editorial manipulation.

The chapter divisions may need a little explanation. The headings of "Just Plain Funny," "Bizarre," "Heart-wrenching," and "Serious," among others, are hardly the normal ways of classifying a narrative. However, I feel that they accurately reflect their contents and I will leave it to your judgment as to whether such departures from accepted nomenclature are valid.

When I eventually hired some paid assistance to help with the trade development at the consulate, I always told the new employees that I could not possibly prepare them for the weird and wonderful stories they would hear and the strange requests they would receive. Almost to a person these new employees thought I had probably been out in the sun a little too long—it was written in their eyes—but they all came to realize that the reality of their daily work was often far more bizarre than I could possibly have described.

I therefore offer the following as an unsolicited accolade for the anachronism known as the honorary consul system. A system that works amazingly well, produces better results than many career diplomatic posts, and provides an endless supply of unbelievable stories for cocktail parties. All at a price, I might add, that even the British government can afford. And to those of you who might think I fabricated them, or just some of them, I can only say that I wish I had that sort of imagination. I don't. To repeat myself, "You couldn't make this stuff up if you tried!"

I always took heart from a lovely turn of phrase from Sir Winston Churchill. He said, when asked to define bureaucracy, "It is a discreditable advertisement of administrative infirmity." If a British prime minister can say that, who am I to take bureaucracy seriously?

As a final thought, if an enlightened British official (an oxymoron if ever I heard one) decides to make this book required reading for all new honorary consuls, or perhaps even for real ones, I should be most grateful. In addition, I would say to that potential audience that your diplomatic experiences will most likely be at least as entertaining and satisfying as mine. In particular, I would add that the position of honorary consul is unique, if anomalous and anachronistic, and you are privileged to receive the appointment. Enjoy it and "*Nil carborundum illegitimi*."

CHAPTER I
A TASTE OF STORIES TO COME

CONSULS A'STRIPPING

"My inspired challenge was three laps of the pool—naked!"

Kentucky colonels and honorary consuls have something in common: They are both anachronisms. This may explain why several honorary consuls in San Juan were also Kentucky colonels.

Kentucky colonels are appointed by the governor of Kentucky under a right that goes back to the U.S. Civil War. The Governor at that time was permitted to form his own militia and that power has been jealously guarded ever since. (The fact that many people in the southern states of the United States still don't want to admit that they lost the Civil War, or even that it's over, may have something to do with this.)

The Governor of Kentucky holds a formal ball in his official residence every year on the night before the running of the Kentucky Derby at Churchill Downs and all Kentucky colonels are cordially invited. There are also worldwide gatherings of Kentucky colonels each year on race day itself. These gatherings are designed to raise money for charity.

There are many famous Kentucky colonels including Winston Churchill, John Glenn, who was inducted while he was in space, and, of course, me.

San Juan, Puerto Rico had its own chapter and the celebration each year of the Kentucky Derby was religiously enjoyed by colonels, wives, and guests. When I was first asked to join this illustrious group it sounded a bit like sedition. How could I represent the United Kingdom and be in the United States military, albeit a somewhat ancient regiment? Surely that was a conflict of interest at best and treason at worst. I was assured that my nomination was quite proper. After all, Winston Churchill enjoyed the honor for many years and his ranking in the British government was slightly higher than mine!

Kentucky colonels' celebration of the Kentucky Derby has four main goals: The consumption of mint juleps, the watching of the race, the enjoyment of a southern meal, and the raising of money for charity, all strictly in that order. (After several hours these priorities tend to concentrate on the first of these goals!)

During my first appearance as a colonel, rather than just a guest, I was volunteered to run "the book." "The book" was the system of betting on the race, and it was this betting that produced the funds that were donated to charity. (Why they thought I knew how to run a "book" I have no idea!)

Normally very few horses run in the Kentucky Derby. Certainly there were more punters in our group than horses to be chosen. Several people therefore ended up putting bets on the same horse. Small trophies were given to the backers of the first three horses to finish and, if there was more than one winner, a choice had to be made because there was only one trophy for each place.

On the year in question three punters picked the winning horse. As guardian of "the book" it fell to me to decide how to break the tie. I asked the three winners for ideas but they were no help. So I tried to think of a suitable challenge—enter, my inspired idea for determining the winner! (But remember this was several hours into the mint juleps!)

I consulted the ladies present and they enthusiastically agreed to judge the challenge. They selected their judges and all stood expectantly waiting for the game to begin.

The home where the celebration was held sat in a lush forest environment, which featured a spectacular view over the city of San Juan. It also featured a swimming pool. My inspired challenge was three laps of the pool—which was about thirty-five feet long—naked. The challenge was duly announced together with the names of the judges.

One winner, an architect, immediately withdrew to great derision from the gathered throng. The other two competitors approached the edge of the pool and started to strip—more cheers from the crowd. Both of the competitors were honorary consuls representing European countries. The consul representing the more northerly country of the two flamboyantly peeled off his shirt and looked around for appropriate accolades. However, the first thing he saw was his compatriot down to his briefs. He froze, thought for a moment and then decided to withdraw. That left a single winner and he did not even have to perform the challenge, much to the disappointment of the crowd and, in particular, the judges.

Terrible goings-on in the colonies! My mother warned me what happens to people when they go to hot climates, although I don't think she factored in the delights of mint juleps! I shall have to be more careful with my inspired ideas in the future.

Can you imagine the headlines?

CHAPTER II
INTERPRETATION
OF THE ROLE

I started my own consulting company in Puerto Rico in 1979 and one of my targeted areas for business development was the introduction of more British goods to the Island. At that time there were very few such imports and those that did exist seemed to have arrived more by accident than by design. It looked like a good business opportunity and, in retrospect, it certainly has been.

The first step was to find out how it could be done. Bringing an individual product wasn't too hard but how could I develop a more comprehensive approach? No one seemed to know.

I spoke to someone in the British Embassy in Washington whom I had known many years before. He had been a commercial officer in the former consular post in San Juan, which closed in 1975. Even he was not sure how to go about it so I decided I would take the plunge anyway. I organized a trade mission from Puerto Rico to the United Kingdom.

That step apparently raised my profile in certain quarters as well as, I'm sure, raising some diplomatic eyebrows. "Who the hell does this person think he is?" I could imagine them saying. However, something obviously registered somewhere because I subsequently received an inquiry asking if I would consider becoming British Honorary Consul.

The inquiry sort of filtered down to me without any formal exchange of letters. That should have warned me how the system worked but I was naïve and, of course, flattered, which inevitably subjugated my reason and logic. "I would be delighted," I said, "as long as it does not interfere with my business interests." After all they were not offering to pay me just offering to give me work and a title; the flattery did not cause me to lose all my reason!

No, I was assured, the position would not create any conflicts and, indeed, if my business and the consulate had related interests, it was to everyone's benefit. That sounded remarkably enlightened (another ominous signal I missed), so how could I refuse?

Much later, when some of the euphoria had evaporated and I had heard nothing further from the government, I idly began to wonder what an honorary consul actually did. After pondering this for some time I decided to ask the people who had offered me the position. Sounds like a perfectly reasonable approach, right?

There was a confused sort of silence and much shuffling of feet. Obviously no one knew the answer to this horrendously difficult question. Further, they gave me the impression that my inquiry immediately started them wondering about the wisdom of appointing someone who would ask such a ridiculous question. In the end they simply ignored it and continued with my appointment process.

Many months later I did get an answer during a lunch in New York with a senior consular official who was a Scot. I don't know if his origins have any relevance but, over the years, I did get more interesting answers from Scots in the diplomatic service than from any others. Usually irreverent answers, it is true, but certainly more interesting ones. The official summarized the qualifications of an honorary consul in the following five points. An honorary consul, he said, should be:

1.   Over sixty-five years of age.

2.   White-haired and carry a stick.

3.   Independently wealthy and able to throw large cocktail parties both at the drop of a hat and at his own expense.

4.   A close friend of the royal family.

5.   A leader of his community.

I'm not joking. That's it, what he said word for word, and since he was the only one to even attempt to give me an answer, even if he made it up, I had to believe it!

Well! I'm pleased to tell you that I did not come remotely close to meeting any of those requirements at the time. And, fifteen years later, I still don't; except that the age of sixty-five, the white hair, and the stick are all creeping up rapidly. I have to wonder why they had appointed me. My best guess at the time was that they were hard-up for candidates. More recently, the facetious part of my mind has taken over and suggested that, perhaps, they made a mistake. The wheels of the Foreign Office do turn rather slowly and it would probably have taken about fifteen years for my papers to clear through the personnel department. The mistake was corrected when they retired me!

That reminds me of something I once said in a similar vein as part of a speech welcoming a British Trade official to Puerto Rico. I explained to the audience of senior Puerto Rican government officials and business people that the last serious British trade mission to visit the island had returned to London and reported that there was definitely a market for British interests. I pointed out that this current visit was the British government's response to that report. After a suitable pause, I added that the original market report had been written by Sir Francis Drake, and this only reflected the normal response time of the British Foreign Office. I doubt whether that gained me many brownie points with the British bureaucracy but it did produce a burst of wry laughter. The fact that the mission leader's name was also Drake added to the amusement.

All of this shows that the British government was hard pushed to come up with an explanation, let alone a job description, for an honorary consul. It therefore falls to me to humbly offer a definition.

I will first return to Graham Greene's book in order to set the tone for the definition and job description of an honorary consul. In the introduction he describes what he used as background for the novel and therein lies a testimony to the importance of honorary consuls. He said:

> Of Uruguay I knew nothing and the Tupamaros were far too efficient an organization to make the mistake of kidnapping an unimportant English honorary consul in place of an American ambassador. Paraguay was quite another matter. Under the heavy rule of Stroessner no guerrilla organization had been able to grow, and it seemed plausible that a small inexperienced group working across the border into Argentina might make the blunder which I needed for my story.

The story being that of kidnapping an honorary consul. Further on in the introduction he continues:

> On the main news page [of the local paper El *Litoral*] I read what was very nearly the story I had come there to write—a Paraguayan consul...had been kidnapped in mistake for the Paraguayan Ambassador and a demand for the release of political prisoners had been delivered to General Stroessner, who was on a fishing holiday in the south of Argentina.
>
> A few days later the General replied to the kidnappers that they could do what they liked with their prisoner—he wasn't interested in anything but his fishing—and the consul was released and forgotten.

Not only was the consul of no interest to the government, he was obviously of no interest to the guerrillas either. The least they could have done was shoot him!

Therefore, if Graham Greene, ably assisted by Michael Caine and my own fifteen years of hindsight, provide an introduction to the *prestigious* post of honorary consul, what then is the definition of the post and attendant job description? I tender the following as a modest contribution to the Foreign Office's personnel records.

The job of honorary consul is the most comprehensive, but most bureaucratically insignificant, of all the positions in the British Foreign Service. No other post has to accommodate quite the variety of situations that an honorary consul encounters with virtually no backup. You receive no training and yet you are expected to flawlessly perform every duty from ambassador to receptionist. And flawlessly, I might add, means flawlessly in the interpretation of both your host country and that of the British government system. I will leave you to guess which is more difficult and frustrating to deal with!

Specifically:

1. *You must maintain the highest integrity at all times.*

You are, in some ways, more accountable than "real" diplomats because you are a long term member of your community. Like it or not, you and your country become synonymous in the eyes of the local population. I find that is still true even five years after my retirement and five years after the establishment of a full diplomatic and trade post in San Juan. You can't escape!

2. *You should be an "ambassador" for both your home and host countries, always remembering where your priorities lie.*

The ugly word "treason" might enter into the picture if you do not remember these priorities. However, it's not easy. "Real" diplomats are moved frequently to avoid such issues.

3. *You should be able to make decisions about a wide variety of situations, from the relatively normal to the bizarre, without requiring assistance from a myriad of meetings, conferences, or even guidelines.*

This gives new meaning to the old phrase, "Making it up as you go along." However, if you can't do this easily and seamlessly you will quickly become sixty-five years old, be white-haired and be possessed of a stick. Maybe that's what the official in New York was trying to tell me!

4. *You should be pleasant and sympathetic in all situations you encounter no matter how idiotic, serious, or banal they may be.*

This is probably the most difficult requirement to meet but an important one since you have to deal with every problem at all of its levels. There's simply no one else to blame things on.

5. *You should be an effective and amusing speaker who can be "on stage" at all times.*

Most "real" diplomats do not have to "perform" until they have had years of diplomatic training and experience, and, even then, many have the support of aides and speechwriters.

6. *You should be a skilled listener.*

You may be called upon to listen to tourists who have lost all their belongings and money but, equally, to a murderer who you are required to visit in the local penitentiary. This latter duty was a bit nerve-wracking the first time when they left me alone in a room with a person who had committed multiple murders.

7. *You should be able to deal effectively with the press.*

Again, "real" diplomats either have specially trained people to do this for them or, in the case of the top ranks, they receive extensive training on how to survive such encounters. Failure means facing tomorrow's headlines that read, "British Consul condemns…!"

8. *You must be administratively accountable to your "home" offices.*

Some, if not the majority, of requirements imposed on you administratively were not designed for a one-person post. The results can be frustrating, overwhelming, and just plain stupid at times.

9.   You must be available for a seemingly endless series of official functions.

Many of these are not all that much fun and some are downright boring. However, someone has to keep all those distilleries running and consular corps around the world make a supreme effort to help. My stock reply to comments concerning how many times my picture appeared in the local papers was, "It's an occupational hazard!"

Strangely enough, much of this description comes quite close to what I was told by the official in New York when I started. So maybe he wasn't so far off after all.

I deliberately left the most important part of the job description to the last. It is the following:

10. You should have fun in the post.

If it isn't fun most of the time then make it fun and to hell with the bureaucrats looking down their noses—or better still don't tell them, although that does tend to spoil a large part of the fun.

I will paraphrase an old saying by way of introduction to the final statement of this job description: "Just because you are being facetious, doesn't mean what you're saying isn't true."

As an honorary consul, since they don't pay you, they can't actually tell you what to do. They will certainly try but, apart from reducing your rank (impossible to get any lower than 391st on the diplomatic ladder), reducing your pay (50% of zero is still zero) or actually firing you, there's not much they can do. And, since firing you would involve actually making a decision, that occurrence is highly unlikely, if not impossible, unless you do something totally reprehensible.

Again, "*Nil carborundum illegitimi.*"

CHAPTER III
JUST PLAIN FUNNY

The four stories in this chapter have the common theme of bringing a smile to my face whenever I remember them. In some cases they did not make me smile at the time but, in retrospect, they are among my fondest memories.

"Musical Planes" relates the hilarious background to an unexpected royal visit to Puerto Rico. The evolution of the arrangements for the fleeting and unofficial visit bordered on farce. However, all's well that ended well, albeit with one minor hiccup.

"Boys in the Club" began with what I thought was a crank call, and ended generating much laughter. We all know how idiotic governments can be at times and this is the perfect example of bureaucratic enthusiasm unfettered by common sense.

"All in the Same Room" relates an incident that took perhaps thirty seconds from start to finish. However, it is necessary to place those thirty seconds in context and to relate the aftermath. The incident remains my favorite whenever I want a private chuckle.

Many event organizers become so wrapped up in the theme of the event they are staging that they forget the practicalities that can make or break the event. "The Joys of Protocol" is but one example of many that I could have chosen. I will admit that I have often fallen into the same traps myself but that does not detract from the amusement of the case.

Please feel free to smile as openly as I do when I remember these experiences!

Musical Planes

"You have nowhere to go but down."

I received a call from a Royal Air Force logistics officer in the U.K. who informed me that a plane of the Queen's Flight would shortly be arriving in Puerto Rico. He added that a second plane of the Queen's Flight would follow some days later and some people would disembark from the second plane and board the first. My first reaction was that surely it would be easier if they did that in London, then they wouldn't have to send two planes, but who was I to question an RAF officer.

I should, perhaps, explain that the Queen's Flight is a special unit of the Royal Air Force that maintains and flies the planes that the Queen and other members of the royal family use when they are traveling on official government business. These planes range from transcontinental jets to a fleet of helicopters.

The officer then wanted to know where he should tell the pilots to put the planes on their arrival. I almost asked if my apartment would do. It is quite large but, then again, not really *that* large, so I suggested that the airport might be a good idea. "Where is the airport in Puerto Rico?" he asked. The RAF was sending two planes of the Queen's Flight across the Atlantic and the logistics officer in charge was asking me where the airport was!

This somewhat inane conversation went on for some time until it became obvious that what he was really doing was asking me to decide what was going to happen. There was no mention at this point of who might be on the planes, by the way.

I decided that the planes should land at the San Juan International Airport and that the transfer should take place in the Puerto Rican Air National Guard base, which is located in a corner of that airport. Hopefully the pilots would be able to find an international airport and the National Guard base gave the advantage of tight security. I explained all this and the RAF officer seemed relieved. He said we would probably talk again nearer the time and that was the end of the conversation.

A little while later I received a call from an official in Buckingham Palace to tell me the Queen and Prince Philip and a staff of forty-two people would transit San Juan in the near future and that they would be changing planes during that transit. I was further told that all necessary arrangements would be made and if there was anything I needed to do I would be informed in due course. The official from Buckingham Palace also emphasized that it was not an official visit to Puerto Rico. They were merely using the airport as a convenience for changing planes. Consequently there should be no publicity.

The Queen was coming to Puerto Rico and I was supposed to sit and wait until something went wrong and then argue that it really wasn't my fault—they had to be kidding!

I called my boss in Miami who had no idea what I was talking about and so passed me up the chain of command—Miami, Atlanta, New York, Washington. None of those posts had any idea what I was talking about either—wonderful. They all, however, suggested that I wait to receive further instructions. Why was I surprised, I thought? It wouldn't be their necks if the planes landed at different airports. Typical. Bear with me it gets better; much better.

I contacted the Puerto Rican Air National Guard to request the use of their base for parking the planes and performing the transfer. (I always think the acronym for the Puerto Rican Air National Guard—PRANG—is wonderful!) They were most courteous and quickly agreed. They asked about refueling and crew requirements as well as a series of perfectly reasonable logistical questions. At this point, I naively thought some sort of normality was entering the picture. I should have known better.

I went out to the base and met the commander who introduced me to all the appropriate staff. They were all very helpful.

The commander and I had an interesting conversation about the possibility of providing the Queen's Flight with an escort into the base. We thought that his squadron of F-16 fighters escorting the royal plane into San Juan might provide a nice touch. I have to admit here that this was really a devious attempt on my part to obtain a free ride in an F-16 trainer. Unfortunately it didn't work. It was eventually decided that the Queen's Flight pilots, let alone the passengers, would not be too pleased if they were buzzed by several F-16s, no matter how friendly they might be. So much for my free ride, but it was definitely worth a try, you must admit. The PRANG Commander was certainly all for it.

The next problem was the secrecy requirement. The airbase would provide adequate security but I could just imagine what would happen if the Queen landed on Puerto Rican soil and I hadn't informed the local government. Hanged in the main square of Old San Juan, perhaps, or banished to the dungeons of the 450-year-old El Morro fortress seemed distinct possibilities. And I could just imagine the response of the British government if that happened: "Spend money for a punitive gunboat action just to rescue an honorary consul? You have to be joking."

No, I decided, I had to tell the governor and the Department of State regardless of what London said.

I won't bore you with the endless discussions about who could come out to the base to see the Queen, who could meet her in a reception line, where they might find a red carpet and who might be allowed to have a cup of tea with her and Prince Philip while the staff changed planes. Suffice it to say that agreement was finally reached although the local protocol chief did not speak to me for several months afterwards. I had committed the heinous offence of refusing to allow large numbers of politicians and friends to attend. Perhaps I should add that there is nothing unusual about such problems, I am sure all diplomatic personnel everywhere encounter similar monumental issues when official visits take place.

Finally the day arrived for the first plane to land. I had managed to find out by then that the first plane would be a small one because the larger VC-10 that would bring the royal party across the Atlantic was too big to land at most Caribbean airports. And the smaller one could not make it across the Atlantic without stopping. Thus they were "staging" the smaller jet in San Juan. I mentally apologized to the RAF officer with whom I spoke initially for having thought it would be easier to handle the transfer in London.

I also learned, to my horror, that the San Juan stop was the beginning of the Queen's first official Caribbean tour for many years. If I got it wrong, the whole tour timetable would be in jeopardy. I suddenly knew what they mean when they say you have nowhere to go but down.

I went out to meet the pilot and crew of the small jet and spoke to them as they were "bedding it down" to await the arrival of the VC-10 two days later. I thought I was seeing things. They were actually polishing the outside of the plane by hand, would you believe. The pilot informed me that we had to transfer eighteen of the forty-two people on the VC-10, together with their luggage, to his HP 185 within a forty-minute window.

He then informed me that all planes of the Queen's Flight have their main doors on the left-hand side of the fuselage—doesn't everyone know that? That means, if you think about it, that it is impossible to park two of them with the main doors facing directly across from each other without the almost certainty of tearing a wing off when they move forward. And jets don't back up very easily.

You may well be wondering at this point where on earth I am going with this story. You may also be yawning so I'll stop and start another one just to keep you awake.

"Boys" in the Club

"He authorized the placement of a recruitment ad in the publication The Pink Paper, *which is London's top gay paper."*

Government agencies are not generally known for their good sense, or even for their common sense, and the British government is no exception. However, this story goes well beyond the bounds of credibility.

The phone rang one day and the caller asked, in Spanish, for the application forms to join MI6, the British Secret Service. Of course I had the forms immediately available!

Joining the British Secret Service by applying to an honorary consulate in Puerto Rico. Better chalk this up as another story for the cocktail party circuit, I thought! The caller was quite insistent but, since I had absolutely no idea what he was talking about, I merely said I would investigate his request with our offices in New York and call back. After hanging up, I realized that the caller's voice had rather a distinct tone although I didn't pay much attention until I received another similar call also asking for the same forms. The only real difference was that this second call, which came in a few days later, was carried on in broken English.

I answered the second call by saying that, while I knew nothing about it, I thought it extremely unlikely that any country would openly recruit non-citizens for its secret service. However, I would investigate and call back.

You see I was again demonstrating how good a bureaucrat I had become—never answer a question and always offer to call back but never do so!

However, I decided that two such calls in a short period of time coming from what appeared to be the same segment of the society deserved further investigation. If nothing else it might prepare me for a better response to possible future calls. I called my boss in Miami who passed me on to the Consulate General in Atlanta who passed me on to the Consulate General in New York. My associate in the New York office burst out laughing. Another nutty call from that honorary consul in—where was it again? Oh yes, Puerto Rico, I imagined him thinking. But no, he actually knew what I was talking about and proceeded to explain.

Sometime earlier, the British government, as part of its redefined non-discrimination policies, had decided that gays were completely eligible for government positions. I don't know why they bothered, there were always plenty there to begin with. As a result of this new policy, some over-zealous and none-too-bright personnel director in MI6 (now there's a theoretical oxymoron if ever I heard one) decided that this new policy should be formally implemented. All in the interest of more open government I presume. He authorized the placement of a recruitment ad in the publication *The Pink Paper*, which is London's top gay paper.

Apparently there is considerable communication between the gay populations in London and those in New York, and also between those populations in New York and those in San Juan. That issue of *Pink*, with its MI6 recruitment ad, made its way to Puerto Rico and my callers were actually answering a legitimate inquiry!

The arrival of the magazine in New York had also produced a flood of calls to the British Consulate General there—they must have heard of the British Secret Service's reputation. Hence the laughter at my inquiry.

I wonder how many other gay populations around the world received copies of that issue of *Pink*?

Back to the San Juan Royal visit.

MUSICAL PLANES—CONTINUED

"There went my knighthood in one easy step…"

We left the story with the crushing dilemma of how to arrange the planes so that the transfer could be expedited while, at the same time, not creating a situation that might result in damaging the aircraft.

The PRANG ground controllers became involved and offered suggestions, which rapidly led nowhere. It seemed as though it should be a simple problem, especially for those trained to move planes around, but apparently not. The expression on the face of the pilot of The Queen's flight mirrored my thoughts: Neither of us really believed this was happening or, more correctly, not happening. I decided to act. You see, I had not become a true bureaucrat.

I said we should move three of the F-16s out of the way, place two, one on either side of the apron approach, and move the Hercules into the hangar. Oh! The power! But I forget myself. The centre of the apron should then be cleared of all ancillary equipment. The Queen's flight pilot and I then had a short discussion. We asked for some chalk, which was forthcoming. We walked out onto the apron and drew two large crosses on the ground. "We'll put the nose wheel of the small plane on this cross," we said, "and the nose wheel of the large one on the other cross over there." The National Guard officials looked a bit blank so I said to the pilot, "Go and get your plane and put it on that cross and they should get the idea." He did and they did.

The really amazing part of all this was that they all actually thought I knew what I was doing! I then told the PRANG officials that no one was to touch or move anything until the royal party's arrival (you see, power really does corrupt!)

The great day arrived and everyone turned out in their best uniforms and finery. At the last minute I discovered that the local officials had brought a truckload of antique furniture from their offices in Old San Juan. It looked a bit out of place in the operations room of a fighter base but I suppose it was better than asking the Queen to sit on a folding metal chair.

A beautiful spread of cakes and savories had been provided for tea and the order of precedence in the receiving line introductions had finally been decided. Everything was set. The VC-10 pilot had even been told, over the radio, where his chalk cross was located. I could relax.

When the VC-10 was a few minutes out, it suddenly occurred to me that I didn't know what I was supposed to do. Should I wait at the bottom of the stairs and be first in the receiving line so I could introduce the local officials? Not really, because that would give me a precedence I didn't rate. Should I go on board and greet the royal party? Perhaps, but if I did, I could hardly walk off with the Queen—even her husband can't do that. I certainly could not come down the steps ahead of her and if I came off after her, I wouldn't be there for the introductions. All this may seem a little trivial, but at such times trivialities loom large and potentially dangerous. As I said earlier, you have nowhere to go but down.

The only person who might have been some help was the pilot of the small jet. After all, he must have gone through this before. "I haven't got a clue," he said. Wonderful! He then gave me a brilliant solution that I would never have thought of in a million years. True, I swear. "Why don't you go on board and ask the Queen how she would like you to handle it," he said. I can't do that, I thought. But what the hell—it was a sensible solution. There was no time left and I couldn't think of anything better. So that's what happened.

After boarding the plane and greeting the royal party, I came off and waited at the bottom of the stairs to make the introductions. Amazingly simple!

(I've almost finished I promise.)

The Queen and Prince Philip disembarked and, after the formal introductions, they were escorted over to the operations room for tea. The royal staff rapidly set about transferring the luggage and everything appeared to be going very smoothly— definitely an ominous sign. The planes were in the right place, the luggage and the people were moving, I had remembered the names of everyone in the receiving line, including my wife's, and the air-conditioning in the operations room was actually working. A cup of tea and I could relax.

Prince Philip remarked on the delightful spread of cakes and pastries and proceeded to sample them. The conversation was becoming less stilted when I happened to turn around. A waitress was handing the Queen a cup of tea in a cup that must have weighed a pound, with a rim that was at least an inch thick, with a teabag in it with the string hanging over the edge.

There went my knighthood in one easy step.

Nowhere to go but down!

"…imagine what the London tabloids would do with such a story!"

Political correctness, and the avoidance of anything that could even remotely be interpreted by the media as suspect, has come to occupy a major part of all government officials' thinking. Their public image has to be kept so squeaky clean and if this image were actually true, imagine how they would be: Not only immensely boring, but also totally unimaginative. Maintaining a successful balance between public reality and real reality becomes an all-consuming game.

Relations between political rivals are governed by the general rule that you need to have at least as much dirt on them as they have on you. A dynamic balance is struck and each side understands the game. However, dealing with the media is a different story. If you are a public figure you have to treat the press as if they were malicious, vindictive, liberal with the truth, sneaky, and generally untrustworthy. (Not a bad job description for many of them, come to think of it.)

It is absolutely a love-hate relationship—you can't live without them and they can't live without you but you both spend your time trying to destroy the other. Occasionally, it is tempting to think, at least at the level of true politicians, that they really deserve each other.

When amusing and slightly suspect incidents happen to public figures, as they inevitably must, those incidents have to be enjoyed in private with one eye looking over your shoulder. An example follows.

The visit of a British minister to Puerto Rico was always special. On this occasion it was to open the new offices of the Honorary Consulate. Honorary consulates rarely merit the visit of a regular consul let alone a minister of state from the Foreign and Commonwealth Office in London, so this was quite unusual. However, there were extenuating circumstances.

The minister concerned had a particular interest in the Caribbean and had been instrumental in creating the Honorary Consulate in San Juan. In the years since the establishment of the post we became good friends and remained so until her untimely death a short time ago. I hope, therefore, she would not mind me sharing this story; in reality, I know she is still chuckling about it.

British ministers tend to travel with just one person accompanying them. Often, they travel completely on their own. This is a constant source of amazement to Puerto Rican Government officials; even Island mayors of quite small towns never go anywhere without a collection of drivers, bodyguards, and aides.

In this case the minister was traveling with an old friend of mine. He and I had originally met when I was first trying to bring British products to Puerto Rico, long before I became honorary consul. In fact, it was only because of his efforts in London that the post was established at all. At the time of the visit he was heading a "quango," which is a peculiarly British term for a quasi-government agency. In his case it was an organization that received most of its funding from the government, advised the government on policy issues in the Caribbean, but employed non-government workers. Thus the visit to San Juan was official but also low-key since I knew both visitors well.

I met the minister and my friend at the airport and drove them to the hotel. One nice thing about being an honorary consul is that you can go through to the gate to meet VIPs and escort them all the way out of the airport. This does mean, however, that in meeting international flights you actually leave the country for a short while and you normally have no documents. Fortunately, I never had any trouble getting back in. The local consular corps used to joke that this procedure presented an excellent opportunity to have an unwanted spouse deported with no blame falling on the conspirator but I never heard of anyone actually trying it.

A British company managed the hotel I had chosen and they had agreed to give the minister an upgrade to the executive floor (heaven forbid that the British government would actually *pay* for something like that.) When we arrived we were whisked up to the top floor of the building for special check-in. The receptionist welcomed us and asked the minister to fill out the appropriate registration forms for a room. My friend and I stood aside and waited.

As the minister started writing the receptionist looked up and said, "Will you all be in one room?"

The pregnant silence was broken by stifled attempts to hide our laughter. The receptionist looked nonplussed. She obviously had no idea what she had just suggested and proceeded to ask the question again!

The minister later told me that she woke up several times that night chuckling and trying to imagine what the London tabloids would do with such a story. "Minister Dallies in Exotic Caribbean Island" might have been one of the kinder headlines.

The memory still brings smiles to our faces years later and, to my knowledge, the incident was never leaked to the press.

The Joys of Protocol

"…we got home several hours later, still steaming both figuratively and literally."

One of the joys of protocol is that it often requires you to do the most stupid things without complaint while, at the same time, looking as though it's all perfectly normal. Depressingly, the later part of that statement is quite true—most of the time it is quite normal in a twisted sort of way.

However, on such occasions you are representing your country and therefore have to dress and behave accordingly. This usually means sitting in uncomfortable chairs that are too narrow (even for my slim figure), over-dressed for the climate, and having to listen to interminable, usually boring, speeches. If you are lucky, you can then grab a quick drink, sample the hors d'oeuvres just in case you get stuck there for longer than you expect, and then quietly disappear as soon as you can. Unfortunately, those in charge of such ceremonies have learned how to combat this strategy and have designed theirs to keep you from leaving for as long as possible. (I confess I learned this as well when my own functions were involved.)

If you are in charge, therefore, you start the ceremony as long after the announced starting time as possible and you don't open the bar or serve the food before the speeches. Cruel and unwarranted punishment if you are on the receiving end and perfectly justified planning if you are on the giving end. Sometimes, however, unpredictable events occur which lighten the atmosphere a little. Here is one such example, although I have to admit it was only funny in retrospect.

The inauguration of a governor in Puerto Rico is always a grand affair. In this particular case the organizing committee decided to hold the official ceremony on the grounds of the historic El Morro fort. This is a large grass area on the landside of the fort, and is bordered on both sides by the sea—the fort itself guards the San Juan harbor entrance. The area is usually blessed with a good breeze and in winter it can be very pleasant. However, eighty-four degrees Fahrenheit in the shade may be fine for flying kites—a major pastime of the local citizens—but its appeal changes somewhat if you are wearing a dark suit and sitting still.

On the occasion in question, we arrived to find that the chairs for the VIPs were out in the open with no cover. Worse, although we didn't realize it at the time, the chairs were placed at right angles to the direction of the sun. There was little we could do about it since all the VIPs, including the governor and his cabinet, were in the same position. Perhaps the person in charge of the organization thought that "open" was a practical reality that reflected a political statement. People organizing such events do crazy things sometimes in the name of different, or politically correct, themes.

We baked in the afternoon sun for about two hours waiting for the start of the ceremony. Finally, the Secretary of State rose to begin the program. No sooner had she started speaking than we were treated to a tropical shower. I should explain that tropical showers sometimes dump as much water in five minutes as many hurricanes do in their entire passage and this was one of those. The secretary was drowned. Hair bedraggled, makeup running, and clothes completely soaked, she bravely persisted in her speech. As soon as she had finished the sun came out again and the humidity went through the roof. I was so glad I had worn a dark suit—but not a three-piece one, thank god.

When we got home several hours later, still steaming both figuratively and literally, we discovered we had a unique temporary memento of the occasion: bright-red, sunburned faces—but only on one side! We looked beautiful.

I really will not miss such protocol occasions!

CHAPTER IV
SERIOUS

I debated the wisdom of including a "serious" section in this book. I concluded that it would be remiss if I gave the impression that everything the consulate did had a funny side. Much of the work produced significant results and many of the incidents were positive contributions to Britain's promotional efforts in Puerto Rico. In addition, the work was a source of personal pride and satisfaction over a fifteen-year period.

You will notice, from the Table of Contents that the chapter heading "Serious" appears six times. That is because there is only one story in every "Serious" chapter. To have placed them all together would not have maintained an effective balance. The approach may be a little different but I hope you enjoy that difference.

I will begin with a remarkably sensible and simple idea which proved to be of enormous value to the war on drugs in the waters of the Caribbean. The "Ship Rider" program was operated jointly by the British Virgin Islands Police Department and the United States Coast Guard based in Puerto Rico, and later extended to include the Dutch Coast Guard in the Caribbean.

Further "serious" chapters include the following: "Cuban Refugees" documents an evolving saga of miscommunication, or more accurately no communication. The likely outcome could have been disastrous without the input made possible by a chance meeting that took place several years earlier.

"Made in Puerto Rico" is an excellent example of the vagaries of U.K. customs law. The situation took over a year to resolve and involved everyone up to the level of the U.S. Ambassador to the Court of St. James.

"Normal Consular Work" attempts to portray the type of work honorary consuls perform on a daily basis. Some of it is humdrum, some of it is exciting, and some is bizarre. The balance is interesting.

"The Jaguar Dealership" follows the quest for the establishment of an official dealership in Puerto Rico. It is an example of what to expect when dealing with large corporations and, also, what can be achieved by pure bloody-minded persistence.

Finally, "Hurricane Hugo" provides a series of anecdotes set against the background of one of the most destructive storms in the world.

SHIP RIDER

"…approval usually took three hours to reach the ship's captain."

Much of the drug traffic coming north from South America uses Puerto Rico as a gateway into the United States. The flights from San Juan to the mainland are classified as domestic and therefore not overseen by U.S. Customs.

Puerto Rico is one hundred miles long and thirty-five miles wide and is surrounded by beaches. It also has numerous short airstrips that were built for crop dusters and small private planes. Many of these are now semi-abandoned. Puerto Rico is only a few hundred miles from the north coast of South America, an easy hop for a small plane. The island has a modern road and motorway system that makes internal movement extremely quick and easy.

Marine traffic, both commercial and private, is heavy between Puerto Rico and the British and U.S. Virgin Islands, which are located thirty to fifty miles to its east. In other words, there is an almost endless variety of ways to land drugs. Equally, therefore, the area is difficult to patrol comprehensively if you are trying to stop such drug shipments.

The British Virgin Islands has over thirty-six islands scattered over fifty-nine square miles. It is a very difficult place to patrol consistently and well. Small planes, flying low, can easily drop watertight bundles into the sea and then quickly disappear. The local traffickers, using small boats, then recover these bundles. The bundles make their way to Puerto Rico and so onto the U.S. mainland. The BVI police force has patrol boats but providing an effective shield around the whole area is virtually impossible.

The U.S. Coast Guard maintains a major presence in the area and a significant part of their time is spent combating the drug traffic. It has a fleet of several 110ft cutters, smaller boats, long-range helicopters, a Hercules transport, and an executive jet packed with electronic detection equipment. It also has a contro-versial ground radar system that can see several hundred miles into the heartland of South America. This system was originally designed for the Cold War and was based in Guam to monitor Russian aircraft movements, but it is very effective at pinpointing small drug planes.

The two services have worked together for years but they often encountered a major interdiction problem. When a U.S. Coast Guard vessel, in pursuit of a suspected drug boat, reached the border of British Virgin Islands territorial waters, it had to stop and radio in requesting permission to enter those waters. The drug boat, of course, did not bother with such niceties and rapidly disappeared over the horizon. The request for permission was routed from the vessel to the Coast Guard base in San Juan, to the 7th Coast Guard District Headquarters in Miami, to U.S. Coast Guard Headquarters in Washington DC, to the U.S. State Department, through the British Embassy in Washington, and so on to London. The reply followed the same route back to the vessel. I should add here that the BVI is a British territory and so the U.K. has sovereignty.

Amazingly enough, considering this convoluted bureaucratic routing, the entire approval process usually only took about three hours or so to reach the vessel's captain. However, by then, the drug boat was long gone.

After many years of frustration over this legal restriction someone, and I don't know who, came up with an amazingly simple solution. I wish I knew who that someone was because he or she deserves a medal. The solution was to place a BVI police-man on each U.S. Coast Guard vessel and a U.S. Coast Guard officer on the BVI police launch. In that way the sovereignty issue vanished since the correct jurisdictional officer could make the arrest. What a great and inspired idea! It was called the "Ship-Rider" program.

Currently, the program is even more effective. It has been extended to all British territories in the Caribbean and there is no longer a requirement for British policemen on U.S. Coast Guard vessels or U.S. Coast Guard officers on British police launches. The regulations have been changed and either group has the right to enter each other's territorial waters and make arrests. A similar arrangement is in place with the Dutch–Caribbean Coast Guard Services.

Unfortunately, when efforts were made to export this brilliant idea to the rest of the Caribbean, local politicians killed the initiative. They complained that such a program would violate the sovereignty of their islands. It is tempting to ponder their motivation.

CHAPTER V
BIZARRE

Bizarre is the best word I can think of to describe the following stories. Each has its own unique twist and they have provided an endless source of amazement to all who have heard them.

"Keystone Cops—Caribbean Style" is a candidate for another Michael Caine movie about the Caribbean with, perhaps, John Cleese as the captain of the police launch. The story still amazes me today, many years after the event.

"The Celtic Baron" is one of those stories that you wouldn't believe no matter who told you. I have to assume that this individual is still wandering around the world creating bizarre incidents wherever he goes. I'm sure it must be good for his security business. You can hardly fail to remember his visit.

"Burial at Sea" can be bizarre, sad, infuriating, and amusing, depending who you identify with in the story. It is probably not the only case of its type but it seemed to fit well with the other stories in this chapter.

"The Anglo-Saxon Chronicles" really is bizarre and there's no other way to describe it. In a way it's a shame it had to end in the way that it did—all offices need a little distraction from time to time—but the possible security implications meant it had to be formally investigated.

Finally, "The British Consul's White Flag" is funny and bizarre.

I'm not sure I have forgiven the governor for what he did to me even though we've often shared an amusing conversation about the incident.

KEYSTONE COPS—CARIBBEAN STYLE

"Put a shot across their bows."

This story began shortly before the visit of a Puerto Rican governor to the United Kingdom. It was the first time a governor from the Island had paid an official visit to Britain and so anything that could possibly have a negative impact on the trip had to be treated with great caution.

The story also involved a local legislator who was not well-known for his sane approach to conflict, or to anything else for that matter. I might add that he was not directly involved with the governor's trip. He had the reputation of being rather a maverick with many people questioning how many of his cylinders were actually firing. A person, in other words, to be handled with kid gloves. Thus the potential damage that could have resulted from this incident extended far beyond the dubious merits of the case itself. However, the entertainment value of the story more than made up for any concerns of a more serious nature.

I received a call from the office of the local legislator in question. His office manager informed me that a Puerto Rican fishing boat from their political district had been arrested by the police of a British Island in the Caribbean. He then insisted that, since the

Caribbean Islands were British, I was in a position to do something about this obvious mistake. (I must say I always have problems when someone says they "arrested a boat." The U.S. Coast Guard does it all the time in the waters around Puerto Rico but I've never actually seen a pair of handcuffs that big.)

I told the legislator's office manager that I would investigate and get back to him. I called my boss in Miami, who passed me on to New York, who passed me on to the Embassy in Washington—standard procedure when a case is difficult and someone might get blamed for something. Washington suggested that I call the British Governor of the Island. I duly placed the call and was subjected to a diatribe about how little power he really had as governor and how he was not able to achieve anything. I almost offered to send him a violin for Christmas. I was so amazed at this outburst I almost forgot why I had called in the first place. Subsequently, I learned he had a reputation for such behavior— no one I talked to in the British government system seemed the slightest bit surprised by what happened. Don't they have selection processes for these positions? Talking to this paragon of the British colonial administration was obviously not going to get me anywhere, so I looked for other sources of information.

Gradually, over the next month or so, the story came together, and this is where it gets interesting, if you have an appreciation of the ridiculous. First of all it was not a Puerto Rican fishing boat, it was from the Dominican Republic, but it did have a Puerto Rican crew. That piece of information becomes more relevant later. It seems that many such boats frequently fished illegally in the territorial waters of the British territory concerned. The law required them to obtain a license for such activities, but most of them never bothered. It had been going on for years.

The fishing boats had always managed to avoid problems in the past because their boats were much faster than the Island's police launch. When the police launch appeared they would simply pull in their lines and disappear over the horizon. It had become a rather silly game. However, several months before the incident in question, the British government had bought the police a new fast patrol boat with a gun mounted on the bow—I thought they had given up gunboat diplomacy years ago, but I guess tradition dies hard.

On this occasion, the boat concerned was fishing illegally as usual when the new police patrol boat appeared. The fishing boat crew duly hauled in their lines and took off, only to find the police launch overhauling them. Quite a surprise! The police launch drew alongside and, using its new high-powered loudspeaker system, ordered the fishing boat to stop. The Puerto Rican crew replied appropriately, or inappropriately depending on your perspective, and kept going. The police captain grinned (my embellishment) and, in ringing tones, ordered his gunner to "Put a shot across their bows." The fact that this was the first time in his life he had ever been able to issue such an order merely added to the excitement. The gunner lined up his new gun and fired. Unfortunately, just at that moment, the patrol boat hit a small swell. The round went straight through the flying bridge of the fishing boat missing the captain by inches. I don't know what the Puerto Rican captain said, but I could take a reasonable guess, and this book would probably be banned if I repeated it here. The fishing boat stopped and was arrested—those big handcuffs again.

The police secured the fishing boat and towed it back to the main harbor Islands. Just as they reached the police pier, the Puerto Rican captain decided that things were getting serious and he wasn't about to sample the delights of the local jail. He slammed the throttles wide open, snapped the tow rope, managed to slice about six feet off the end of the police pier, and hastily departed for more hospitable climes. The police boat again gave chase and, of course, caught up again. "Another shot across the bows" was the command. Only this time the round did actually go across the bows. Back to the police pier they went. The crew were handcuffed—instead of the boat this time—and thrown in jail.

The next morning the crew was arraigned in front of a local magistrate, who they attempted to bribe. Pundits might say that not enough money was offered but, whatever the case, the crew went back to jail to await trial. A week or so later they appeared before a judge to answer the multiple charges against them (too long a list to reiterate here, but you can imagine). During the trial, the local consul for the Dominican Republic appeared and testified. I can only imagine that the fishing boat owner instigated petitions that resulted in this testimony. In any case, part of his testimony involved offering a bribe to the judge to let the crew go (I'm not making this up, I swear). One is tempted to again listen to the pundits because the judge sentenced the crew to a long term in jail.

At that point this bizarre story apparently came to an abrupt halt until I initiated inquiries on behalf of the Puerto Rican legislator. My contact in the British Embassy and I agreed that this was our chance for fortune if not fame; write it up and sell the script to Hollywood. We would only have to add a few sharks and a female love interest and it couldn't fail!

I don't know what happened to the local Dominican consul but he might have been well advised to arrange a hasty departure from the reach of that judge. The Island police are probably still using the confiscated boat and I have heard no more about the prisoners. I did manage to pacify the local Puerto Rican legislator and the gubernatorial visit to the U.K. proceeded without any repercussions from this incident.

The Celtic Baron

"I do pay a little closer attention to the policemen patrolling on my street now."

My son was a teenager at the time of this story and it was his interest in local nightlife that introduced me to this bizarre saga.

The owner of one of the top nightclubs in San Juan called to ask my advice on dealing with a strange situation that had occurred on her premises the night before. She said that a group of seven men carrying guns had come into the club and told the management that they were the advance party and bodyguards for "The Baron." The management, she said, explained in the strongest possible terms that no guns were allowed anywhere near the club under any circumstances. The bodyguards insisted that their principal was an official

British government representative and he didn't go anywhere without his full security detail, who were always fully armed. They said "The Baron" was a guest of two members of the United States Army, who were also present. The balance of the bodyguards were local policemen. She let them in.

Shortly thereafter, "The Baron" himself appeared dressed in full Celtic regalia, including a claymore. He demanded Irish whiskey and, having consumed two glasses, he left and took his entourage with him. The last bodyguard to leave informed the owner that "The Baron" would be back the following night and that appropriate arrangements should be made. The owner called me to ask what those arrangements should be.

Needless to say, I had never heard of "The Baron" and the whole episode sounded so unlikely that, if I hadn't known who was calling, I would probably have thought it was a hoax. However, under the circumstances, I said I would investigate.

I should quickly add here that, in my experience, British officials never travel with bodyguards. Top officials might have a private assistant but that's about it. In the few cases where the British Ambassador in Washington visited San Juan, for example, he came completely on his own. The idea that anyone would need seven armed bodyguards just didn't make any sense. And the idea that a British official would parade around in full Celtic regalia was just too ludicrous to contemplate. I've met some pretty strange ones but not *that* strange!

I was now faced with an interesting dilemma. I had promised to investigate but how could I ask the necessary questions of my bosses in New York without them thinking I had finally lost it completely? A parallel situation bailed me out. I knew that the former President of the Soviet Union, Mikhail Gorbachev, was due in town the following evening to give a speech. It crossed my mind that someone posing as a British official with armed bodyguards, at precisely that time, could certainly have major security implications. This turned out to be doubly worrying when I discovered Mr. Gorbachev was staying in the hotel where the nightclub was located. Here was the reason I needed to cloak my questions to New York in an aura of credibility. I called the Consulate General and initially met with the response I half expected. When they stopped laughing, they did some checking and no one had ever heard of "The Baron." They told me to alert the local authorities and the FBI, which I did. However, although this helped, I had promised the nightclub owner a quick response to resolve concerns should "The Baron" return; besides, my curiosity was getting the better of me. Who was this apparent fraud? I called the hotel where "The Baron" was supposed to be staying only to be told he was not registered. Perhaps I had reason to worry! I called the nightclub owner and reported what I had found out so far and promised to continue the investigation in the morning. I then went off to some official function before going home.

That evening, about nine o'clock, the phone rang and it was "The Baron." That's how he introduced himself. He said he'd heard that I was trying to contact him and wanted to know why. (It didn't occur to me until afterwards to wonder how he got my home phone number. But more of that later.)

I explained to him what I had been told by the nightclub owner and then, in the nicest possible terms, I asked him who the hell he was and what the hell he was playing at. He proceeded to explain that he was Baron Castleshort and that he was "one of the Celtic Barons from Ireland." He claimed that he always wore traditional dress and, furthermore, that he was Director General of the International Bodyguard Association. This association, he claimed, was based in London and trained bodyguards all over the world. He was in Puerto Rico to inspect the local chapter's courses and practices. I had heard some tales over the years but this struck me as one of the better ones!

He then proceeded to try and intimidate me with his list of contacts and clients. Even to the point of stating that he had accompanied the Duchess of York on her recent trip to St. Petersburg. It did occur to me that he must actually believe in all this himself because no one would have the gall or the imagination to make up such a ridiculous story. It might even be true, I thought.

His next comments were a little more sinister, particularly in light of his knowing my home phone number. He said he was working closely with the local Puerto Rican police, many of whom were graduates of his school, and that he had a meeting in the governor's residence the following morning. In the process of this explanation he let slip that he knew my home address, as well as my home phone number. Perhaps he had sent "his" local police to watch my apartment. Was it coincidence that he called me within minutes of my arrival home? Paranoia, perhaps, but as the saying goes, "Just because you are paranoid doesn't mean they aren't out to get you." The conversation continued in this slightly inane way with him trying to intimidate me and me trying to be polite. When we hung up, I looked up the International Association of Bodyguards in the telephone directory. It existed in Puerto Rico but when I called a child answered who said her father was out with a foreign guest.

The following morning, on my way to the office, I turned on my car radio and found myself listening to "The Baron" being interviewed. The story he told was the same as the one I'd heard the night before, which made me feel a little more comfortable. After all, if he was here for nefarious reasons, he would hardly advertise the fact by giving radio interviews. But then you never know.

The episode fizzled. Mr. Gorbachev made his speech without incident, and both he and "The Baron" apparently departed safely. I did half-heartedly try to track down the association in London with little success. However, the internet provided an extensive website on "the Lordship of Castleshort." The title, according to the website, could be traced back to 1390. It also stated that the present "Lord of the Barony" was, among other things, an active member of the International Association of Chiefs of Police. Perhaps the whole episode was legitimate after all, although it was certainly a bizarre way of acting under any circumstances. Needless to say, I do pay a little closer attention to the policemen patrolling on my street now!

Burial at Sea

"It would have been interesting to have been a fly on the wall when the real wife stormed in after her return home."

One of the strange duties of consuls is to certify dead bodies. At least, I was often required to certify those that had died aboard cruise ships that docked in San Juan Harbor. Towards the end of my consular tenure this apparently gruesome task was supposedly abolished, but some ship's captains still insisted on its performance. In any case, despite my initial trepidation, I didn't actually have to poke around in the coffins to make sure the bodies were, in fact, dead—the ship's physician had already done that. All I had to do was witness the official death certificates and the ship's log entry. Such duties almost always occurred on Saturday mornings since that was when the majority of cruise ships arrived. They happened surprisingly often but, I suppose, over-indulgence and an aged population, which tend to characterize people on cruises, must be a bad combination.

(The people from Cunard shipping lines once told me that the largest supply items—in terms of volume—that the *QE2* carries on her round the world cruises are empty coffins. Charming! Aren't you glad you know that?)

I have to admit that I did not directly witness the following story. It was related to me, and confirmed, by an officer of the cruise ship in question. I cannot totally corroborate the details, but it perfectly matches this chapter and certainly is no more bizarre than any of the other stories, all of which I know are true.

One of the deck officers of a cruise ship greeted me one Saturday morning with a story that makes you both chuckle and feel sad. However, in overall terms, bizarre is a better description. The officer told me that one of the passengers on a previous cruise had died of a heart attack one night. It was a massive attack and there was nothing the ship's doctor could do to resuscitate the victim. The captain and the crew expressed their condolences to the man's wife and everyone treated her with the utmost kindness for the rest of the trip.

The captain reluctantly told the widow that the appropriate papers had to be filled out and asked if she would mind working with the chief purser on the details. The widow agreed and then mentioned that it was always her husband's wish to be buried at sea. She said that she was slightly distressed by this wish but, under the circumstances, perhaps it was for the best. The captain said that such a request was certainly possible and arrangements could be made. The widow concurred.

When all was in order the captain presided over the burial

service and, with all due ceremony, the man was buried at sea.

The ship finished the cruise and, just before they docked, the captain asked the widow if there was anything he could do to assist with her return home. She was grateful but said that everything had been arranged and she would leave the ship normally when everyone else disembarked. After the docking procedures were complete, early on the Saturday morning, all the passengers disembarked and, by around 9:30 A.M., they were all gone. About an hour later the officer of the watch noticed a lady standing at the bottom of the gangplank. He watched her for some time and finally walked down to ask if he could help in any way. "I'm waiting for my husband," she said. When she gave the officer her husband's name he blanched and asked her to come on board and wait in the lounge for a few minutes. He rapidly called the captain who then had to gently break the news to the lady that her husband had been buried at sea. Not an enviable task.

After the shock had worn off, everyone had but one question. Who was the other wife? Now I would suggest that anyone contemplating a cruise, accompanied by someone they are not supposed to be with, should pay close attention at this point. All cruise ships, as far as I know, take thousands of photographs of their passengers during each trip. These photographs are displayed in the main lounge each day and the passengers are encouraged to pay outrageous prices to purchase copies. You can generally avoid this ritual if you keep a sharp eye out for the ubiquitous camera people. However, there is one exception. Everyone has their photograph taken as they come on board when they first embark. So if you are contemplating an illicit caper, make sure you don't board together! Back to the conclusion of the story.

After inconclusive attempts to identify the bogus wife, one of the officers suddenly remembered the photographs taken on arrival. The negatives were quickly found and, after several hours of searching, the lady recognized the other wife. It was her husband's secretary.

I thought, afterwards, it would have been interesting to have been a fly-on-the-wall at the office when the real wife stormed in after her return home. The mind boggles at the possibilities of such a confrontation but I guess we'll never know what actually happened. Maybe they both celebrated!

No lawsuit was apparently brought against the cruise line, which was somewhat surprising, but they had acted "in good faith," I suppose. A sad story and also a funny one, in a macabre sort of way. But perhaps just simply bizarre.

THE ANGLO-SAXON CHRONICLES

"God safe [sic] the democracy."

I now that the United Kingdom Nations (Great British, Ireland, United States, New Zeland) need betters infantries weapons because the United Kingdom nations lose the secrets wars from Spain, Japan, Germany, Russia, Italy, France, Portugar and more nations.(sic)

For this reasons you can not lose time, soldiers, opportunities, money, industries, technologies, sales, commerces. I go to say that you need for infantry a betters helicopters, and fracmentaries bombs by relists. (sic)

So starts a letter that is reproduced in full below. The letter was received somewhere towards the end of a saga that developed slowly over several years until the circumstances went beyond being amusing and became a little sinister.

It began with an anonymous hand-written letter that said the forces of evil were upon us and that we, the Anglo-Saxon race, should band together for our own survival. The forces of evil were identified as Hispanic, although that interpretation required more than a little deduction from what was actually written. It did seem a little strange that the letter, although in English, was obviously written by someone whose first language was Spanish. The constructions were all wrong and some of the words were obviously bastardized. However, the contents of the letter were so bizarre that errors of spelling and grammar paled in comparison with the overall impact.

THANK YOU FOR SEND THE
BRITISH PRIEST FOR SAVE ME SOUL
OF THE DAM OF SPANISH SPIES AND PRIEST.
THIS CHRISTMAS GO TO BE THE MORE
HAPPY OF ME LIFE. THIS SAXON PRIEST
OF GREAT BRITISH IS SAINT AND SAY
THAT HE PUT ME SOUL FREE OF THE
SPANISH PRIEST, THANK YOU FOR SAVE
ME SOUL. GOD MOST SAVE THIS PRIEST.
GOD SAVE QUEEN ELIZABETH AND
PRINCESS CHARLES.
    THE SPANISH ARE VERY RASIST TO
THE SAXON RACE AND THE JEWISH RACE.
BECAUSE TRUST IN THE CAPITALIST
SISTEM. I AM COMMUNIST WHO NOT
BE RASIST AND I GO TO PUT A PARTY
CALL DEMOCRATIC WORKER CAPITALIST PARTY.
I AM OF THE SAXON RACE AND I NOT
TRUST IN THE SOCIALIST MOVEMENT
BE-CAUSE IS RASIST. THE PARTY GO TO
BE OPEN IN THE YEAR 2010 IN WASHINGTON
D.C. BECAUSE I AM POOR AND I CARE ABOUT

The letters continued to arrive over a period of years with no
particular regularity. They gradually became more voluminous
but rarely departed from the central theme of decrying the
Spanish persecution of Anglo-Saxons. The letters became a part
of the office life and we almost looked forward to the next one.
They were an amusing distraction.

I have reproduced part of the first letter here and, in it, the
author makes mention of someone sending a priest to see him.
Not guilty!

I am saxon race and DARKWING say that the saxon race belong to the
Great British Territories and the anglo race not want the saxon race
in Great British and the International Socialist organizations give
right to saxons race go to live in Great British but you say that the
saxons are's criminalas for use others language names.
    Let my give my problems that I am saxon race and I have spanish name
and I can not change this name never in Puerto Rico by laws. The
spanish goverment say in the schools a long time ago that if we have
other race not latin but have a talk perfects spanish not have problems
with the latins race. The problems was the things that say the anglos
race went say if not have an english name not belong to Great British.
I want to go live to Great British but I not have english name and I
think to change name in Great British if I found a job(any type) but
a teutonics race want to do same of my self for destroy may sale of
a Cyclotron for Devopment of Antimatters.
    I want to help the saxons race in Great British and in generals
meannings all the people of the United Kingdom but this teutonics
are supposts to be in Russia but I think that not be reals the things
that want to do because not want to be with the Teutonics russians and
I want to now if you go to take this teutonic man for I go to the
Swiss or Norway for make the proyects of the Cyclotron Developments
of Antimatters for I not waste my time.

                                        Thank you for your time;

The letters did not appear to be a security risk and I'm sure
most diplomatic posts receive similar correspondence at one time
or another. I should add that no attempt was ever made to contact
this person directly. Neither, to my knowledge, did he ever
attempt to telephone or contact the office other than through his
letters.

After a year or so of these periodic missives, a new aspect was
suddenly introduced: "The Nose" as it came to be called. The
author suddenly started signing off with a drawing of a nose:

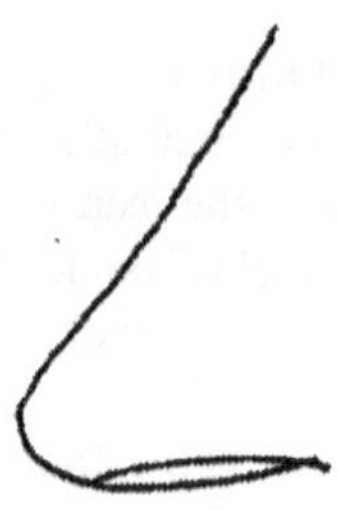

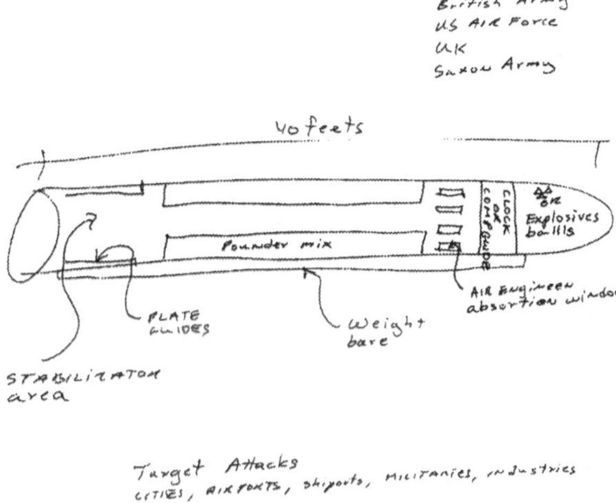

I did not have the faintest idea what "the Nose" was supposed to mean but the caricature was repeated on all subsequent correspondence. It also, by popular office consent, became the name of the case file.

As the months continued to pass with more letters arriving I noticed a change in atmosphere. Whereas before, the office staff obviously thought it was funny, they now began to think that every crank call and strange visitor was "the Nose." We certainly had our fair share of crank calls and strange visitors so it became a concern. It was at that point that he began to add another twist— we were obviously fertile territory, from his point of view.

He began sending us "blueprints" for offensive weapons that he had designed. As illustrated above.

United Kingdom Consulate
Suite 1100
1509 Lopez Landron st
San Juan PR 00911

    I am saxon race and I come from Spain of the province of name Lion
and we have a lot of racials problems with the latins, morons and
teutonics anglos arians nordics in Spain because this province was the
must develop in industries before the secound war and the first war and
the civils war. The progress was destroy by the knife of the priests
and some's say that the Lion province was part of the United States
and the United Kingdom. The people of the provice of Lion want to go
to live to Great British because the Lion is the symbol of the british
king. The pyramid in the United States means that not live arians in
this nation and the eagle means the saxons color race like the lion
the saxons color race.
    We have a lots of problems with the province of castilla because feel
under develop and want to say that germany progress more and the same th·
anglos of the develop of Great British and that was the problems with
the spanish. For that reasons I want politicals asylums in Great British
for develop the cyclotron of developments of antimatters in peace for
build the ship call UK TITANIC of speed of 5140 light years/hr.
The picture steals the name.
    You have big problems with the spanish because the spanish say that
United States belong to Spain and not to Great British and you in
secrets ssend to make the exterminations of the people of the province
of Leon using the change of name's unlawfuls without autorizations of th
peoples of the province of Leon. For this reasons you must give my the
politicals asylums in Great British because I born in Madrid and I have
criminals in United States who steals the patents of the cyclotron
of developments of antimatters.

                              God safe the democracy;

He also appeared to have acquired a typewriter during this period
so his letters became a little easier to decipher if no easier to
understand. On reflection, if I had understood them I would have
been the one in trouble!

The designs he sent were for "bullet-proof helicopters",
special fighter jets and rather strange artillery pieces.

```
United Kingdom Nations
Suite 1100
1509 Lopez Landron st
San Juan   PR   00911

     I now that the United Kingdom Nations(Great British, Ireland, United
States, New Zeland) need betters infantries weapons because the United
Kingdom nations lose the secrets wars from Spain, Japan, Germany, Russia,
Italy, France, Portugar and more nations.
     For this reasons you can not lose time, soldiers,opportunities, money,
industries, technologies, sales, commerces. I go to say that you need
for infantry a betters helicopters, and fracmentaries bombs by relists.
I go to show how you can have a betters infanties weapons.

                    Helicopter specifications

     Proofs to bullets of M-16, M-60, K-47 the structures
     of the helicopters.

     Must use eight(8) screw propelers for get speeds of close
     to the #1,000 km/hr.

     Good visions windows of the helicopters for see the infantry
     men on strategics military positions.

                    Fracmentary bombs

     The fracmentary bombs consists of a hollow zinc half
     sphericals structures.

     In side the fracmentary bomb have BB's of .177 cal buy to
     DAISY CO and CROSSMAN CO

     In the secound interior have a half shericals explosives
     of black pouders or plastics(three time more explosive to
     black pouders)

     Over all this have a parachutes for the helicpter go out
     of the area and for give time to the detonators.
```

When he suggested that he was going to send them to the British government for evaluation, I had to really do something about it. He would probably have said I told him to do it, which would have been another "Brownie point" on my illustrious diplomatic record. However, before I could act he apparently sent the ideas to the Canadian government. He wanted to know about starting companies and selling shares to build these weapons. Would you believe the Canadian government replied, passing him to another department? If you don't believe me, read below, the referral is on the top.

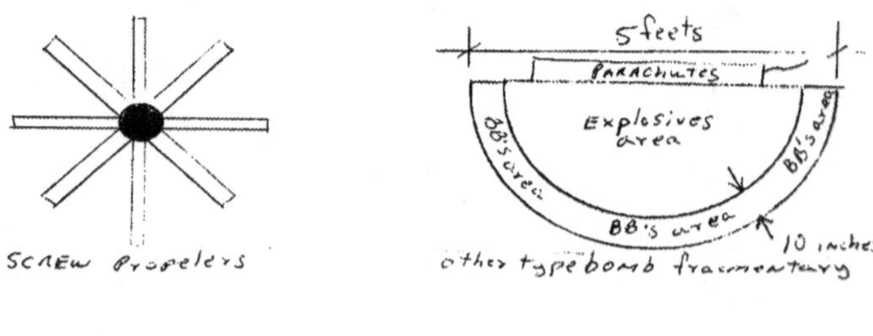

Refered to Industry Canada.

Public Information Offices
Library of Parlament
Parlament Hill
Ottawa, Ontario
K1A   0A9

I whats information about the department of stocksholders markets of Canada, because I whats to open an industries of fighters bombers aircraafts with the sales of stockskolders
If you have this departments for I put the announcements of the sales of stocksholders because I am engineer.
                    God safe the democracy;

IAN COURT
BRITISH CONSULATE
AMERICAN AIRLINES BUILDING
11TH FL., SUITE 1100
CALLE LOPEZ LANDRON 1509
SAN JUAN, PR 00911

DEAR CONSUL COURT:

PLEASE CONVEY THIS MESSAGE TO THE BRITISH GOVERNMENT:

MY PATIENCE IS WEARING THIN. YOU HAD MORE THAN ENOUGH TIME
TO REMIT THE U.S. $3,000.00 YOU OWE ME...

YOU REALLY WANT TO BE CAREFUL. TO OWE ME, IS TO OWE THE VERY
DEVIL. FOR AS GOD IS MY WITNESS, I WILL DO EVERY THING IN MY POWER
TO MAKE YOU AND YOUR NATION PAY WITH HIGH INTEREST..., AND THAT
INCLUDES THE POLITICAL SMEAR. YOU BETTER BELIEVE IT! I HAVE A
25-YEARS RELATION WITH JAPAN THAT GOES ABOVE ANY DIPLOMATIC
INFLUENCE YOU MAY HAVE, AND I, AS LADY DIANNA WILL NOT GO QUIETLY.

I LIKE TO THINK THAT WITH 1997 APPROACHING SO FAST, THE LAST
THING YOUR GOVERNMENT WANTS IS TO TURN MORE ENEMIES IN ASIA
FOR A FEW DOLLARS, ($3,000.00) BECAUSE YOU BETTER BELIEVE, YOU ARE
GOING TO PAY ONE WAY OR ANOTHER.

THIS AMOUNT IS SOMETHING YOU CAN PULL FROM A FUND ANYWHERE,
AND FOR GREAT BRITAIN'S TRANQUILLITY, IS WELL WORTHWHILE.
AFTER ALL, NO ONE DEFEND YOUR NATIONAL SECURITY WITHOUT A SALARY,
NOT YOUR INTELLIGENCE SERVICE, NOT THE MILITARY, AND I AM MUCH
TOO KIND FOR ASKING NO OTHER THAN MY VEHICLE BACK.

I MAKE A DEAL WITH YOU: SEND MY MONEY, AND I WILL RETURN
ALL ENGLISH PUB-GLASSES I TOOK. THIS WAY WE ARE EVEN
AND COULD GET A CLEAN START. YOU REALLY DO NOT WANT TO
LOSE ME AS A FRIEND. I HAPPEN TO KNOW HOW POLITICALLY
INVALUABLE I AM. YOURS WAS NOT THE FIRST REQUEST I
RECEIVED TO TRAIN FOR INTELLIGENCE, JUST ASK AROUND.

YOU HAVE MY WORD FOR IT, NO ONE IS GOING TO SLAP YOUR WRIST
FOR DOING THE RIGHT THING. I KNOW THIS IS NOT THE WAY AGENTS
GET PAID, BUT THIS IS THE QUESTION; I AM NOT YOUR AGENT.
I AM JUST A POLITICAL FIGURE ALL IN MYSELF AND REGARDLESS
OF MY OWN NATIONALITY. CAN BRITONY RULE O.K. THIS TIME
AS WELL? I EVE SEND YOU A POEM FOR OLDE TIMES SAKE:

Finally, and I assume because he had not heard from me, he
began to get abusive as the last letter reproduced here demonstrates.

The appropriate authorities were called and after careful
explanation—there might have been a temptation to believe I was
as disturbed as the person who wrote the letters—the case was

apparently investigated. By this time the file was quite thick and so copies were handed over to the U.S. Federal Diplomatic Protection Service—the relevant agency.

I was kept informed as the investigation progressed and, eventually, was told that the author had been interviewed and persuaded not to bother the office again. I was also informed that he was not considered dangerous. Where have I heard *that* before!

There was general relief in the office but I have to say that, in a bizarre way, everyone involved rather missed "the Nose."

Maybe now that I've retired, I'll send them all a Christmas card with "the Nose" on the bottom!

There is a sequel to this story. I have often wondered what happened to the person who wrote those letters and whether he continued writing them, albeit to someone else.

When this book was in the production process, many years after the original events took place, I was advised that I should obtain a release from the author for the use of his letters and his designs. The advice said that, even though they were written to me, they were still legally under his copyright. If I could not obtain such a release, I would have to take them out of the text.

I searched back through the file with the vague idea that there might have been an address on an old envelope. Of course, if he was using a fictitious name he may well have used a fictitious address although the Federal Consular Protection Service found him. Also, it was years later and he could have moved.

I found an address, located it on a map of San Juan, and drove off to make contact. I found it was inside a "gated" community but one with no guard, just an intercom. Can you imagine trying to explain to someone over an intercom in the middle of the street why I wanted to come in? Fortunately, someone was coming out, so I slipped through the gate before it closed. I found the house but no one was home. Do I leave a note? Again, difficult—how many pages would I need to explain? None of the neighbors seemed to know whether he still lived there or not.

On the third expedition like this—I was getting quite good at slipping through the gate—a lady answered the door.

After a short explanation, she kindly invited me in and introduced me to her daughter. Further explanations followed and they explained that the person I was looking for was the son/brother but he now lived in Philadelphia. Triumph and defeat, all within thirty second. But wait! My son lives in Philadelphia, perhaps he could obtain the signature for me. Hope again.

My hosts were very gracious and explained that their son/brother was a brilliant student when he was younger but that, when he started his second degree in engineering, he had a major mental breakdown from the pressure and never really recovered. They also explained that some of his designs were actually patented!

The mother agreed to contact her son and persuade him that he should sign the release. She saw no problem and said she would call me the next day. Nothing happened—again euphoria to defeat, but this time in twenty-four hours.

A week later I called her—she had given me her phone number so I would have to keep "breaking into" the community. She said that her son was in a delicate stage at the moment and that my request might have a deleterious effect on him. Certain defeat—I would have to rewrite the story or eliminate it. She then proceeded to say that she was his legal guardian and would be happy to sign a release!

I am grateful for her understanding, without which the story would be a skeleton of its original self. I can only wish her and her family well.

"I was left standing there, feeling just as much of an idiot as I probably looked."

The British government has a wonderful program (another oxymoron candidate you may think, but not true in this case) that invites prominent members of other countries to visit the U.K. at Britain's expense. On first sight this may appear to be yet another government junket but it is a program that works extremely well. The program is called the U.K. Visitor Programme and in my time was run by The Central Office of Information or COI.

There are many reasons why the program works well but the most important is that the individual visits are designed around the wishes of the visitor as well as around the requirements of the British government. One of the guests from Puerto Rico, for example, wanted to see King Arthur's Round Table in Winchester, and that wish was accommodated. Certainly my experience, and those of most of the people I have talked to, clearly indicate that virtually all such visitors return to their respective countries having become complete anglophiles. The program is worth its weight in gold to British promotional efforts at all levels. It may be difficult to quantify, and therefore difficult to justify, but it is extremely successful and helpful to those of us on the front line.

The office in London that runs the program is efficient, knowledgeable and pleasant—and it's a government office? Well! Not really. It's paid for by the government but it has its own director general who is appointed for a ten-year period. That effectively takes the position out of the political arena. I mentioned a "quango" in one of the previous stories. This is another example.

What has this got to do with a British consul and his white flag, you may ask? Patience, I'm getting there!

This story concerns the visit of a governor of Puerto Rico to the U.K. To my knowledge it was the first time a political leader from the Island had ever visited the U.K. in an official capacity. Many precedents were to be set and much of the protocol was untested. I should perhaps explain here that a Puerto Rican Governor has a great deal more power than any other U.S. Governor because the position controls the local tax system—Puerto Rico is the only U.S. jurisdiction that is not subject to the U.S. Internal Revenue Code. Thus the visit created somewhat of a dilemma. The Governor was more important, diplomatically, than a U.S. governor but he was not a head of state. COI decided to err on the positive side of this situation, which was why the incident in question took place in one of the British government's main reception centers.

The Governor asked me to accompany him on his visit and I relayed that request to my bosses. I should have expected the reply, which was: "I hope you don't expect the British government to pay for your trip." Well, actually, I did hope, but I should have known better. Still, I could hardly say "no" to the governor, so I paid for myself as I did with all future visits—honorary consuls are expected to be martyrs and/or rich among other things. The governor then amazed me by asking if I would write the speeches he was required to give in London. After checking that I was not about to violate some British government code, and therefore end up in the Tower of London, I did. (In reality I was probably quite safe since an honorary consul certainly would not rate such a high privilege as being incarcerated in the Tower.)

The governor used the first speech I wrote almost word for word. In the second, he used the majority and the third resulted in this story.

The third speech was given during the principal formal dinner. About forty people attended, if I remember correctly. When it came time for the speeches, the governor started off by talking about the relations between Britain and Puerto Rico and then said he wanted to tell a story. (There was no story in my script, but then I was merely the speechwriter.)

He said he wanted to explain certain events associated with the U.S. invasion of Puerto Rico in 1898. In that year, Spain lost the Spanish–American War and Puerto Rico was one of the spoils ceded to the United States. The island had been a colony of Spain for over four hundred years and both the language and the culture were, Spanish; as in many other Spanish colonies, indigenous populations in Puerto Rico had been quickly annihilated. The U.S. was, therefore, somewhat wary of its possible reception when it arrived to assume sovereignty. This was the age of gunboats and marines, and both were dutifully sent to take over Puerto Rico.

I must admit that we, the audience, and me, the co-opted speech writer, were all getting a little nervous at this point— where on earth was he going with this story and how long would it last? I was just hoping it would not produce some diplomatic blunder or result in some protocol faux pas. Speechwriters are given to such paranoia as such times!

He explained that the American troops landed at Guanica, a small town on the south coast. The landing point was about ten miles from the second largest population centre, the city of Ponce. The troops landed, established a beachhead and looked around for someone to fight. However, there didn't appear to be anyone in the immediate vicinity willing to take up that challenge. Somewhat disappointed, the commander ordered a march on Ponce. The troops dutifully marched off, preparing for a fight or, perhaps with any luck, a siege. Just as the troops were deploying to begin their attack on the city, a lone figure was observed walking towards them carrying a white flag. The scouts reported that the person had walked out through the main gates and appeared to want to talk. The American commander marched out to meet the flag.

At this point in his story the governor turned to me and asked me to stand up. I did, but with mixed emotions. I wasn't sure who was going to shoot me first, my government or his.

The governor continued by saying that the person carrying the white flag was, in fact, the British Consul in Ponce. He was carrying a message from the city garrison that there was really no need for a fight because the American troops were all quite welcome.

"So Ian," he said, turning to me again, "you have a great deal to live up to in developing relations between the U.K. and Puerto Rico." And he sat down. I was left standing there, feeling just as much of an idiot as I probably looked. Still, governors must have their little jokes, I suppose.

I have tried, on more than one occasion since, to find out if his description of the incident was true but the truth appears elusive. The governor, of course, still assures me that it is absolutely true. I wonder.

CHAPTER VI
SERIOUS

"It is one of the joys of the position of honorary consul that, since you really are deniable and dispensable, you have the freedom to achieve significant successes at times."

This story could have turned out very differently but for an accidental meeting that took place over a year before the saga began. So a little background is necessary to place the events in context.

A discussion forum, which I organized and still continue to run in Puerto Rico, had chosen as one of its major topics, "What happens after the Normalization of Relations with Cuba?" Puerto Ricans have always been apprehensive about Cuba "opening up" again because the obvious U.S. interest in such an occurrence might divert Washington's attention from their island's needs and aspirations. However, the approach they generally take to this fear is denial: *"If I don't think about it, it won't happen."* Consequently, the topic is rarely discussed openly.

The forum has always undertaken controversial topics and the subject of Cuba was certainly no exception. The purpose of this particular meeting was to probe the possible nature of a post-Castro Cuba and how such changes might affect Puerto Rico.

I asked a close friend, who is a leader of the Cuban community on the island, to either speak or recommend someone who could. He recommended a close friend of his and this resulted in the "accidental" meeting.

The forum itself is not germane to this story except to say that it produced some lively discussion that I thought, at one point, might begin a Cuban civil war right there. Thankfully it didn't, but it did provide a fertile outlet for ideas. The most significant outcome as far as this story is concerned that it cemented a relationship between the presenter and myself that still continues and flourishes today.

About a year later, during one of the periodic waves of people trying to reach the United States from Cuba in small boats, this story began.

Some of the boat people apparently thought that if they went south instead of north they might avoid detection by the Cuban Navy and the U.S. Coast Guard. They crossed over two hundred miles of open water and tried to land on the Cayman Islands. I assume they thought they would be sent to the U.S. Instead the Cayman Island government interned them in refugee camps.

One of the major Cuban exile groups in Miami, the Cuban American National Foundation (CANF), became outraged at this internment and decided to send a mission to the Cayman Islands. They said they were going to document the "abuses" allegedly suffered by the refugees at the hands of the Cayman Islands Government.

It has to be said that certain elements within the Cuban exile community were not exactly known for their restraint and diplomacy and when the Governor of the Islands threatened to refuse the mission's entry, the situation became tense.

The Cayman Islands is a British territory, has a London-appointed governor, and is under the jurisdiction of the British Foreign and Commonwealth Office. CANF obviously understood this since their anger was directed not only against the Cayman Islands and their government but also against the British Consulate in Miami. The situation was rapidly deteriorating but none of the parties were talking to each other. It was a potential bomb, both figuratively and literally.

My Cuban friend was one of the original members of CANF and was well aware of this emerging danger. We discussed the problem and agreed we would attempt to intervene. He would act as the conduit to the Miami group and I would act as the conduit to the British government. (A bit presumptuous on my part perhaps but, what the hell, no one else was doing anything and the previous history of CANF did not suggest that they might produce a thoughtful solution.)

I called my direct supervisor expecting the wrath of God to fall on me. To my surprise, I was told to continue acting as a conduit. However, the more I thought about it the less surprised I became. No one in any position of significance wanted anything to do with the situation in case it blew up in their faces. I, on the other hand, was eminently deniable and, I suppose, eminently dispensable. So I was the perfect person to let loose on the situation. A cheerful thought, but an expedient decision!

The situation escalated to the point where the Governor issued a "line drawn in the sand" statement, literally. It said, in effect, that any boat people attempting to land on Cayman beaches would be returned to the sea. This inflamed the feelings in Miami and there was a real risk of some physical damage to the consulate there. In addition, there was some talk of storming the Cayman Islands; many members of CANF had fought in the Bay of Pigs debacle, so this was not an idle threat.

My friend and I managed to keep the communications channels open and a compromise was eventually agreed. A less-radical mission from CANF could visit the camp in the Cayman Islands, with the local government's approval, and could meet and interview the detainees. When they arrived they found that the conditions, while not perfect, were quite good. The refugees were being well treated and the only major complaint was that no plans seemed to be in place to send them to the U.S.A. A potentially explosive situation had been defused and my neck was safe for the time being.

Having avoided what could easily have been a small war, we relaxed. However, the story did not stop there. Further weeks of discussion resulted in the refugees being transferred in small groups to the U.S. Navy base at Guantanamo on Cuba. After processing they were moved on to the Bahamas and, finally, on to Florida. In Florida they were welcomed by CANF, who supported them and found them jobs. They had finally achieved their goal although in rather a circuitous fashion.

One interesting point I learned during this final step was that CANF has never permitted any Cuban refugee it sponsors to cost the U.S. government a penny. A fact that somewhat offsets its more public image of firebrand behavior.

There was one particular and funny story to come out of this saga. Some of the Cuban boat people who landed on the Cayman Islands were reported to have stolen a local boat in an attempt to make for Belize on the Central American mainland. They were successful. The funny part was that the boat they stole had the same name as the Governor of the Cayman Islands' official launch. Some frantic checking followed since public exposure of such a loss, not to mention the security lapse (imagine the headlines!), would have been publicly embarrassing. As it turned out, it was another boat but the possibility did produce some amusement, though not, I suspect, in the Governor's office.

On reflection, I think my friend and I achieved a great deal. Probably more than any regular government officials could possibly have done in the timeframe required. It is one of the joys of the position of honorary consul that, since you really are deniable and dispensable, you have the freedom to achieve significant successes at times.

Finally, and unfortunately, I have to add that the lessons of this story have not been learned. As far as I know, there are still no communication links between the British government and the Cuban groups in Miami. Who knows, maybe I'll be dragged out of retirement one of these days!

CHAPTER VII
LAUGH RATHER
THAN CRY

Crying doesn't achieve very much and generally makes you feel bad. Laughing may not achieve very much either but at least you feel good. This chapter has four examples of laughter winning out over what really should have been crying situations.

"Passing the Radio" highlights the security arrangements for Baroness Thatcher's only visit to Puerto Rico. The visit was conducted under a terrorist alert but the terrorists had no need to bother. The security cover proved quite capable of inflicting serious damage without any outside help.

"Two Events at Once" is difficult to believe. How a group of people, who are sworn to defend their country and its citizens, could be thrown into confusion by simple logistics is a little frightening! How they could leave a British minister standing on an empty pier is amazing!

The last two stories are examples of bureaucratic stupidity at its best. "The Coat of Arms" and "Filing is a Priority" both document situations that are as amazing as they are idiotic. Unfortunately, they are by no means unique.

Passing the Radio

"…IRA machine guns, bombs and bazookas—and his battery was flat!"

Margaret Thatcher was invited to make a speech to the World Forum in San Juan. The World Forum is a local group that specialized in inviting world leaders to address an audience at a special dinner held in their honor. This event occurred long after Lady Thatcher's retirement from parliament and was part, of an international speaking tour arranged by her educational foundation.

A visit to a British company was requested as part of her program and one of the major pharmaceuticals plants on the Island was delighted to help. The plant was located about forty minutes outside of the metropolitan area and that enabled Lady Thatcher to see something of the countryside during her short stay. The entire visit was under a major security warning because of an alleged IRA threat. The U.S. Secret Service was therefore out in force as was the local police department.

Lady Thatcher asked me to accompany her for the visit to the British pharmaceutical company. A great honor, except I couldn't help pondering what I had done to deserve being prime bazooka bait. However, duty is duty and, as I freely admit, being able to talk to her, one-on-one, for an extended period of time was a fascinating and unique experience.

We left the Caribe Hilton Hotel in San Juan with plenty of time to reach Cidra, the small town where the plant was located. The motorcade consisted of two motorcycle outriders with their sirens blaring and their lights flashing. They were followed by a local police car equally well-endowed with noise and lights, followed by a secret service car—no lights or sirens, thank God—followed by our car. Bringing up the rear was another secret service car followed by a police car and, yes, two more motorcycles. If all that wasn't bad enough, the leading motorcycle escorts were traveling at 25 mph in the outside lane of an expressway. (This was good security? Everyone within a three-mile radius must have heard us coming and, at 25 mph, even a ten-year-old could have hit us if he happened to have a bazooka handy.)

It gets better!

After several miles of this nonsense, I asked the secret service man in the front seat of our car if we could speed it up a bit. We were going to be late arriving at the pharmaceutical plant and we looked bloody stupid riding around at that speed on an expressway blocking traffic. (I didn't actually say the last bit but I probably should have.)

He radioed the secret service car in front for them to relay the message to the two police motorcyclists leading the parade. (Why he couldn't call the policemen directly I had no idea at the time, but I was to find out later.) After a few minutes he turned rather sheepishly to us and said he couldn't contact the car in front because the agent in that car had a flat radio battery. There was a possibility of IRA machine guns, bombs and bazookas—and his battery was flat! Give me strength!

Our agent then called the car behind and told them to get a new radio and give it to the car in front. Meanwhile, we were still trundling along at 25 mph. A short while later a car whistled by us on the inside shoulder of the road and pulled up alongside the secret service car in front us. Windows opened and a new radio was passed across. (I wonder where they practice this stuff?)

Now came the interesting bit. The driver of the car who had delivered the new radio, his baton passing act completed, pulled back over to the shoulder of the road. I presume he intended to drop back to wherever he came from in the first place. However, he was in for a surprise as, indeed, were we. The driver was obviously not accustomed to Puerto Rican driving habits, where the hard shoulder of expressways is treated as a legitimate lane—well, maybe not legitimate, but certainly frequently used. As he pulled over, a beat-up old panel truck came barreling up the shoulder to overtake the blockage we were causing—with our *excessive* speed. The secret service car slammed into the side of the truck. Body panels, hubcaps, and God knows what else went flying through the air and they both disappeared off into the weeds on the side of the road as we sped majestically on at 25 mph. *We don't need the IRA*, I thought, *the secret service is quite capable of killing us without their help!*

When we all calmed down a little and stopped laughing, I, asked the agent in front why we still hadn't changed speed. He called ahead to the other car—the radio was now working—only to report back that the secret service radio frequency was different to that of the police and they couldn't talk to the motorcycles.

We arrived at the pharmaceutical company twenty minutes late.

I have it on good authority that the next day Lady Thatcher's bodyguard walked into the Secret Services offices and announced that a special mandatory training session in "passing the radio" would take place that afternoon on the main expressway through the centre of San Juan. I'm surprised he wasn't lynched on the spot, but his sense of humor did provide an appropriate ending for this soap opera!

TWO EVENTS AT ONCE

"Keep those damn ships out of here, they're not just a bloody nuisance, they're a bloody liability."

I was always trying to persuade the Royal Navy to make more visits to San Juan. Such visits helped my promotional efforts a great deal by showing the flag, reciprocating hospitality, and generally encouraging people to "think British." Unfortunately, one of my predecessors—a real consul I might add, not an honorary one—had once sent a memo to the Admiralty in London saying, "Keep those damn ships out of San Juan, they're just a bloody nuisance."

The Admiralty obviously felt hurt by these harsh words. After all, when have British sailors ever caused anyone any problems in a foreign port? They issued a private directive banning Royal Navy ships from visiting San Juan. As you can imagine, the legacy of this ban didn't exactly help my cause of encouraging more visits.

A British minister was due to visit Puerto Rico. The visit program included a speech and a reception. A perfect opportunity I thought. I called the Royal Navy's Flag Officer based in Barbados and suggested that a Royal Navy presence would add a certain kudos to the occasion. He agreed. Emboldened, I said I needed a worship in San Juan on this particular date. (Oh the power! But I forget myself again.) He called back a few days later and said that, yes, a frigate could be arranged.

I should add here that the Royal Navy keeps what they call a "guard ship" permanently on station in the Caribbean. It's getting a bit old now, as, indeed, are the sailors! No, they actually maintain the station with six-month rotations of several ships. "Permanent" is their description not mine!

I now had a whole worship to play with and I could plan accordingly. I decided to use the helicopter landing area on the stern of the ship as the main area for the functions; the helicopter itself could be a conversation-piece backdrop. I would invite about sixty people for the speech and a hundred and fifty more for the reception. The seating could be set up for the speech and then cleared away to accommodate the reception. The Royal Navy should easily be able to cope with this huge logistical problem—not one of my better assumptions as it turned out.

The arrangements went ahead and all the planning seemed to be going smoothly, which is always an ominous sign. Three weeks before the event I received a note from the ship's captain informing me that he could hold the reception or host the speech, but not both. He said the logistics would not work. Logistics would not work! All they had to do was move a few chairs. And these people are supposed to be defending us? And this frigate actually participated in winning the Falklands War! I was speechless, but I had no recourse with the captain. It was his command and his decision whatever I might think. However, it did create some "minor" problems.

Invitations had already been sent out for the speech and for the reception. Not only was that effort now a total waste of time and money but I had to find another location for the speech. I also had to make sure that the location was close enough to the ship so the guests at the speech could easily join the reception. After scurrying around in a panic, I found somewhere suitable and booked the space.

Of course this didn't really matter since the British government was more than willing to double my budget to cover the event (zero times two equals…?)

The ship's docking arrangements were also changed so that it was closer to the location of the speech. At least the local government was willing to help. We were now on a Monday afternoon with the minister's arrival scheduled for Thursday morning.

Late on Wednesday I received a call to tell me that the ship had been diverted. No explanations, no apologies, just diverted! Visions of a hundred and forty people showing up to a British reception for a British minister all standing on an empty pier flashed through my head. I felt like paraphrasing my predecessor, "Keep those damn ships out of here, they're not just a bloody nuisance, they're a bloody liability." Perhaps the captain knew that this would happen, and, in order to help me, had said he could only host one activity. I would then have to find somewhere else for the other one and that location could double for both activities if necessary. Methinks, however, I am being a little too generous in that thought.

THE COAT OF ARMS

"You have to take your little triumphs where you can!"

The idea that a new job would come with the appropriate support package was something I never questioned when I became Honorary Consul. And, by support package, I merely meant the simple things in life, like official business cards. I knew I was dealing with a government so my expectations were appropriately modest. A supply of business cards seemed like a reasonable request even knowing that the British government had a slight reputation for being cheap. Well, so much for basic assumptions. I was informed that the work of an honorary consul did not warrant extravagances such as business cards. "Why would you need them to represent the British government?" they asked. I would like to have replied, but didn't. Unfortunately, I didn't catch the obvious implication that honorary consuls were not actually supposed to do anything of any consequence that would require business cards.

I pursued the issue and, after much fruitless discussion, I resolved to design, make, and pay for them myself. It's really amazing how quickly government bureaucracy can bring you down to their level by making you waste your energy getting angry at totally petty considerations. Equally, I should have known better than to set a precedent of paying for things myself!

Isn't this interesting?

What should I put on the cards? Well, apart from my name, title and address I should obviously have the same British Government crest that appeared on all official correspondence I received. I therefore, in all innocence, "lifted" the artwork of the official coat of arms from a letter I had received from the Consul General in New York and presented it to my printer.

The cards duly arrived looking very impressive and I began using them on all appropriate occasions. Months later, or perhaps it was years, during a visit to Puerto Rico of a British consular official, I was summarily told off for having the gall to use the official coat of arms on my cards. "No consul is allowed to do that," I was told in no uncertain terms. At that point, having gained a modicum of confidence in my new position, I said, "Why on earth not? What are we supposed to be representing here? Besides, it's one of the best promotional tools we have!"

"Not allowed," I was told.

However, since they didn't offer to replace these scandalous pieces of card, I carried on quietly using the ones I had left. They hadn't paid for them after all—I had. Privately, I reflected that the rule didn't make any sense, but then who ordained that governments were supposed to make sense! When the first set of cards ran out, I replaced them with others of the same design and no one appeared to notice. Even completely petty victories become sweet after a while!

Quite a while later I had a visit from a Minister of State of the Foreign and Commonwealth Office in London. I had learned a little more by then, and tried the joke "The nice thing about being an honorary consul is that since they don't pay you they can't tell you what to do."

The joke became a way of differentiating between officials who had promise and those who were already corrupted by the system. Generally, I found that the higher the rank of the official the funnier they thought the joke. But, predictably, all true bureaucrats hated it.

The Minister concerned seemed to fall into the uncorrupted category so I asked him about the absurd rule relating to use of the official coat of arms. He answered, and I quote: "I've never heard of that, and anyway, it's totally bloody stupid. I will investigate."

True to his word, and this confirmed that he was new and uncorrupted, he checked and found that the rule did indeed exist. Even senior officials were not supposed to use the official coat of arms on their cards. However, he could find no one who had any idea where that rule came from and that piqued his interest. He determined to track down this wonderful example of bureaucratic stupidity.

Much later, he told me he discovered that some faceless wonder in the Foreign and Commonwealth Office, who of course couldn't be identified, had made the rule. No one knew why such a step had been taken—he was probably refused official cards— but word of mouth had made it universally accepted. How many years that nonsense had been going on I have absolutely no idea. Even my bosses in the New York Consulate General thought it was a rule, hence their admonition to eliminate it from my cards.

I therefore claim the removal of this monumental piece of stupidity as my major contribution to the decline of bureaucracy. I know it's not particularly earth-shattering, but then nothing to do with bureaucracy ever is.

You have to take your little triumphs where you can!

FILING IS A PRIORITY

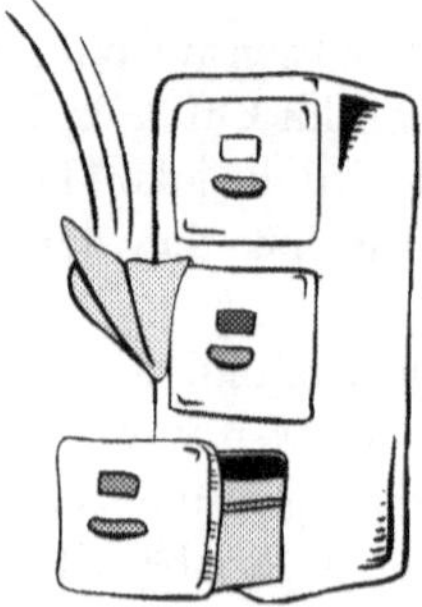

"Those are excellent objectives but I think her first priority should be to get the filing system straight."

If one story in this book typifies the mindset of the much-maligned British bureaucrat then this is it. The example is made worse because the source of the story was a high-ranking diplomatic officer—a consul general no less. I usually found it easy to look at the funny side of bureaucratic stupidities and laugh. This particular one made that exercise very difficult—crying was a much more appropriate reaction.

I made a serous mistake when we first decided that the trade work of the Honorary Consulate in San Juan needed some additional support. I assumed that the person we intended to hire would focus on the development of trade and investment—not only a serious mistake but also a silly one!

On reflection this mistake was probably the beginning of my eventual downfall/retirement. The bureaucracy was never able to accept that a non-paid—and therefore uncontrollable—honorary consul could have an employee reporting to him who was paid by the British government. That just didn't compute and a bureaucracy's normal reaction to anything it doesn't understand or cannot control is to get rid of it, however long it takes. In my case it took thirteen years but that's not all that long in the overall scheme of things. Some may say that I am paranoid to believe such a scenario but, as I have said before, "just because you're paranoid doesn't mean they aren't out to get you."

Now, where was I? Oh yes, hiring some help.

The commercial attaché I contracted was well-known in the community and had excellent contacts in Puerto Rico's business world. It still sounds like a perfect combination to me!

However, in my experience it is quite rare to find anyone who combines a flair for promotion and public relations with good administrative skills. These two attributes seem to require different mindsets and to be good at both almost requires you to be schizophrenic. The person I hired, if she will excuse me saying so, was very good at promotion and public relations, but…!

My mistake was that I did not realize that the primary skill required of anyone working for the British government is the ability to write long, detailed, frequent, and number-filled reports. These reports must be in the correct format so they can be easily counted and then fed into a system (black hole might be a more appropriate description) from which nothing ever emerges. But that doesn't matter, the reports have been counted and marked off on your performance report. Failure to fulfill such requirements means bringing the wrath of the system down on your head—the idea that the quality of those reports might be important never seems to enter the picture. The important issue is to meet the proscribed quota for reports. I swear that, at the end of each month, someone, somewhere, piled all the reports you wrote onto a scale and, if they reached the requisite weight, they sent a little star to be attached to your personnel file. If they didn't weigh enough, that was also recorded. (Sorry, my frustration is still showing even after all this time.)

Finally, it goes without saying that your filing system should be neat and tidy as well as conforming to the government norms. By the way, book actually exists to explain these norms and the corresponding filing system. This whole stupidity was exemplified by a visit we received from the Consul General in Atlanta—he was the administrative boss of the Puerto Rican post. He arrived on the island for the first and only time during his entire tenure and immediately asked me to explain the goals and objectives of the commercial attaché. Nothing about, "Where am I? What makes Puerto Rico tick? Who should I see or how can I help?"—just: "What are the commercial attaché's goals and objectives?" He didn't need to hear mine because I was not an employee (and perhaps it was just as well).

I have to admit that, instead of confronting this monochromatic and unidirectional perspective, to put it politely, I decided to employ the old adage, "If you can't convince them with reasoning, baffle them with bullshit." I sat there and literally made up a list of objectives as I went along. Now I know I'm good at bullshit, but I don't think I'm that good. He should have realized what I was doing. However, he obviously didn't and his reply will stay etched on my memory forever. He said, "Those are excellent objectives but I think her first priority should be to get the filing system straight." *A senior member of the British diplomatic service flies almost two thousand miles to tell me that.* How did we ever build an empire?

CHAPTER VIII
SERIOUS

MADE IN PUERTO RICO

"U.K. Customs Service official declares Puerto Rico is not part of the United States."

I wasn't quite sure whether to tell this story under the heading of "Bizarre," "Amazing," or "Just Plain Stupid." I finally settled on "Serious" because the story demonstrates how obscure legalities can easily and totally ruin good relations and trade between countries. It also demonstrates how bureaucratic and unthinking (are these synonymous?) responses can escalate a minor and relatively simple issue into a major conflict that wastes enormous amounts of time and energy. I therefore offer this story in the naïve hope that it might help prevent future stupidities of a similar nature.

I received a letter from the Puerto Rican State Department concerning a problem of exports from Puerto Rico to the United Kingdom. The letter stated that a manufacturing plant on the Island had sent several container-loads of its products to the U.K. and that Her Majesty's Customs Service had impounded them for false and misleading labeling. That sounded a little strange but little did I know how strange!

I spoke to the general manager of the plant concerned to find out what had happened. He told me that the company produced medical devices and that the plant in Puerto Rico was a subsidiary of a major multinational corporation. The reason the trailers had been impounded, he was told, was that the products were labeled "Made in the U.S.A."

That didn't make any sense because Puerto Rico has been part of the United States since the Spanish–American War of 1898. I know British government agencies are a little slow in updating their information but that was ridiculous. Why were the goods impounded for such an obviously erroneous reason? The manager didn't understand it either but he was stuck with two trailers full of very expensive devices sitting in a dock in the U.K. that he couldn't deliver.

I talked to my bosses in New York and, eventually, to the Department of Trade and Industry in London. They all seemed equally at a loss to explain how this could have happened but, typically, offered no solutions. I decided to ask the U.K. Customs Service direct.

It eventually turned out that a customs officer in the port of Southampton in southern England had decided, pretty much all on his own, that Puerto Rico was not part of the United States. Having made that momentous decision it quickly followed that the goods were mislabeled. They couldn't be made in the U.S.A. if they were made in Puerto Rico.

I couldn't believe what I was hearing. A hundred years or so ago we fought wars over less than that!

In fact it was even worse. Legally, the customs official was perfectly within his rights, and within customs regulations, to make such a decision. I had to wonder where he thought Puerto Rico was, or perhaps he did the same thing with Hawaii or Idaho.

A lowly customs official with the power to decide sovereignty issues governing foreign countries. It sounded like a joke—albeit a bad one.

A barrage of formal letters was exchanged. Bureaucracies love this sort of thing because they hope that, amid all the paperwork generated, everyone will either have forgotten what the original point was or will become so fed up with the lack of progress that they will simply give up or go away. The problem can thus be solved without anyone having to make a decision or sticking their necks out. Hey! Don't knock it, experience has taught them that the strategy works most of the time!

Finally, a formal letter was sent to the U.K. Customs Service from the British Department of Trade and Industry requesting clarification of the decision. We were now nearly six months into the problem. Thank God the goods were not perishable or Southampton docks would have acquired a new reputation.

The U.K. Customs Service reply stated that they had consulted with their lawyers and that this was a clear case of "false and misleading labeling." Obviously, the lawyers were using the same atlas as the original customs officer. Now remember, this is not an individual, a lowly honorary consul or a major international corporation asking the questions at this point, it is the British Department of Trade and Industry. The Customs Service reply was basically telling the Department of Trade and Industry to mind its own business. The mountain growing out of a molehill was increasing in height rapidly!

It always crosses my irreverent mind, at points like this in long-running cases, to ponder the question, "If I could stack all the papers generated so far in this case, how high would it reach?" However, bureaucrats would probably jump at that idea and use it as a performance criterion. The higher the pile the more efficient the administration!

There was obviously nothing more to be gained by confronting the Customs Service. They knew they were right, they were within their law according to their lawyers, and they were not about to listen to any arguments to the contrary. Stalemate! Meanwhile the trailers had been sitting in Southampton docks for over a year.

The Puerto Rican company, in the meantime, had become so totally frustrated they decided to try another route of complaint. Through their parent company they contacted the U.S. Department of Commerce and the U.S. congressman in whose district the parent company was located. The mountain grew a little bigger!

The U.S. Department of Commerce, together with the U.S. State Department, then contacted the American Ambassador to the Court of St. James in London. Now, it really *was* getting out of hand.

The ambassador called the British Foreign and Commonwealth Office. All this because of a decision made by one customs officer in Southampton. It's no wonder that customs officers worldwide are always so officious—they obviously know they have an amazing amount of power and are, literally, a law unto themselves.

The company in Puerto Rico had sent no more exports to the U.K. and everybody was getting more and more upset with everybody else, except on one point—there was unanimous agreement on the need to blow up the U.K. Customs Service headquarters and strangle that customs officer. Not quite, but you know what I mean.

Amid all this chaos, someone, and I wish I could claim it was me, said, "What happens if we label the goods 'Made in Puerto Rico, U.S.A.'?"

Total silence followed with everyone thinking, *That's too simple, it can't possibly work, and if it does we're all going to look pretty stupid.* Well! We all looked pretty stupid and trade now flows freely again between Puerto Rico and the U.K. as far as I know.

I wonder what happened to that customs officer in Southampton?

CHAPTER IX
HEART-WRENCHING

Heart-wrenching can be interpreted in two ways and this chapter has examples of both bad and good heart-wrenching.

"Birth Mother" gives you confidence in the human spirit and the outcomes of positive thinking and persistent effort. It is difficult to imagine that this situation could have worked any better than it did.

"Family Separations" represents the other side of the coin. The story is immensely sad. The real details were not fully revealed during the four years it took to play out but, whatever they were, it appeared that no one was going to win. Least of all the children involved.

"Tribute to Diana" personalizes the worldwide reaction to the tragedy of Princess Diana's death. It revealed how deeply people felt. Even those who had absolutely no connection with Britain or the royal family. The feeling made us all common citizens of the world for a short but memorable time.

"Back to Jail" just made me wish for a happy ending. The case was open and shut but the small human drama was poignant. I hope it worked out, although I haven't heard.

BIRTH MOTHER

"What started as an only child looking for his birth mother ended with uniting three families, a mother and father, seven brothers, and a sister."

Trying to find your birth mother, when many years have passed since your adoption, must be not only an extremely difficult process but also emotionally draining. The highs when you feel you have made progress are, almost inevitably, balanced by the lows when you hit a dead end. The laws involved in adoption generally protect the current family structure and this makes any probe into the original adoption process almost impossible unless someone is willing to bend the rules. This story covered a period of just over a year and involved five countries. However, the complete story began many years previously.

There was a call early one morning from someone who said he was trying to find his birth mother. He said he was calling the British Consulate because one of his relatives had recently revealed that his birth mother was English. I should explain that the consulate, at this early point in its existence, was a phone in one of the bedrooms of my apartment.

If I had taken the call, I would have given the stock answer that the consulate cannot provide investigative services because the system simply does not have the resources or the knowledge. This may sound like a rather callous response to a very sensitive inquiry but it is quite surprising how often such requests are received. If they were all investigated it would absorb enormous amounts of time apart from the fact that consulates do not have that type of expertise. In addition, there was always the possibility that the relatives concerned didn't want to be found and then the consulate would be placed in a difficult position. Unfortunate, perhaps, but realistic.

While it's understandable that the British Consulate would be one of the first logical places to start if the person you were seeking was British, the logistical task of trying to find a single name is overwhelming. There are 60 million people in the U.K. alone and when you add those British subjects living in foreign countries, the numbers become impossible. It would be cruel to raise anyone's hope that success could be achieved.

However, my wife took this particular call and therein lies the story that makes this case very special.

The caller said he was born in Puerto Rico and had been adopted at birth. He was now twenty-nine years old and, until recently, had not even known that he was adopted. When his adoptive mother died a few years previously, one of his relatives told him that his birth mother was English. My wife asked about the circumstances. I'm not sure why she asked because she was well aware of what the consulate could and couldn't do—perhaps it was a woman's intuition. She then asked the crucial question, "What was your birth mother's name?" To her amazement he named someone she had known thirty-five years before. The girl, as she was then, had lived in the same town in England and had traveled out to Puerto Rico with my wife's sister. A year later my wife arrived on the island and they became good friends. The coincidence was amazing.

Unfortunately, the girl had left Puerto Rico only a few years after that and all contact was lost. My wife remembered that there had been a baby and an adoption, but thought the girl had been pregnant before she arrived in Puerto Rico. Something about time spent in Spain before coming out to the Caribbean, but it was all a bit vague. This revelation obviously caused great excitement on the part of the caller but it threatened to be short-lived since the trail had gone cold thirty years before. My wife offered to help.

After checking with all the friends who went back thirty-five years, the only piece of information that surfaced was that the girl had left Puerto Rico soon after the adoption and was thought to have gone to Brazil. That was obviously a dead end since no one was sure where in Brazil she might have gone or, indeed, even if it was Brazil in the first place.

The caller had contacted at the British Consulate after a period of five years of following his own leads. He had begun with the Records Office in San Juan and had finally obtained his original birth certificate which gave him both his original name and that of his mother. He had used those names to search every telephone listing in every major U.S. city. He had found one match in New York who referred him to a genealogist at the College of Arms in England. The genealogist had suggested calling the British Consulate in San Juan.

Once my wife had exhausted her possible leads in Puerto Rico, the only other possibility was to start from the front end and try in England with the family. The girl's family had lived close to my wife's family, although no one could remember the details. Several discussions with my wife's mother produced an address and, during a visit to the U.K., she and her mother went to see the house. The occupants were very understanding but had absolutely no information. Another dead end!

A chance conversation with a friend in England a few months later produced the idea that the girl might have attended Roedean, a famous private school for girls. Such schools usually keep alumnae lists and try to keep them up-to-date. After forty years it was a long shot but worth a try. To everyone's amazement a quick exchange of letters produced a current address in Western Canada. A small town with a small population. It should be easy.

Then, however, came the real dilemma. Would she want to know? Did she have a family? Did they know anything about a baby born nearly thirty years ago? An open approach could obviously cause more problems than it solved and a lot of people could be hurt. However, it would have been impossible to stop at that point.

The man seeking his birth mother was a "medivac" pilot and, as such, flew all over the U.S. on a regular basis. He decided to visit the town in western Canada on one of his trips and just look around. The temptation to go beyond just looking around and to try making contact would probably have been overwhelming, but his mother had moved. She had indeed lived there until recently but had moved on with her family of four boys and her husband who was the local minister. The local post office had the forwarding address. Panic again. Did her family know? If not, would the knowledge destroy a marriage, a family, and a possible relationship with her long-lost son before it could even start? To make matters worse, the husband was a minister and leader of the community. Quite a conundrum!

It was decided that my wife should make the initial contact and try to ease gently into a conversation about the long-lost baby. She decided to make up some story that could be acceptable after all these years and then gradually raise the issue. We all held our breath. The phone call was made and, much to everyone's relief and joy, the mother was ecstatic. The family knew all about the child and they had, in fact, made several attempts over the years to trace his whereabouts themselves. They had encountered the same problems as the son. The records were sealed and their inquiries produced nothing.

Telephone calls were exchanged, meetings arranged, and, to our delight, there was a reunion here in San Juan with the mother, the son, and his four step-brothers. My wife and I were invited. Inspired by his success in finding his birth mother, and with her help, he quite quickly found his biological father in Spain. What started as an only child looking for his birth mother ended with uniting three families, a mother and father, seven brothers, and a sister.

Amid all of the regular nonsense of the consulate it is simply nice to be able to relate such a story.

FAMILY SEPARATIONS

"…the man will probably not see his children until they are adults and able to make decisions for themselves."

Many situations I encountered at the consulate had happy endings but, unfortunately, many did not.

In contentious cases involving family feuds it is almost impossible to determine guilt and extremely dangerous to try. Equally, when a citizen of the country you represent asks for help you have to do your best to provide what help you can. I will thus tell the story as it occurred while acknowledging the fact that most of what I heard was inevitably one-sided.

A British citizen from the Cayman Islands was working in Puerto Rico when he met and married a local girl. They subsequently moved back to the Cayman Islands where they started a family. They returned to Puerto Rico on a variety of occasions, but only for holidays. At some point the wife came back to Puerto Rico to see her parents and brought the children. She did not return to her husband.

Initially she told him she just wanted to extend her vacation but he gradually found it more and more difficult to reach her when he called. She was staying with her parents and they, apparently, always claimed she was out at the time of the call. Finally, they just hung up on him as soon as they heard his voice.

He came to Puerto Rico to find out what was going on only to be handed a restraining order forbidding him to see his wife or his children. After several weeks of frustration, he had returned to the Cayman Islands. Just before he left he hired a Puerto Rican lawyer to represent his interests. It was his subsequent frustration with his lawyer that pushed him to seek my help. He claimed he was completely bewildered by all of this. He and his wife were happily married and they both loved their kids. He could only conclude, he said, that her parents had brain-washed her into believing that she would be much happier with her own family in Puerto Rico rather than living in some foreign country. The only thing I could do was listen and offer to assist in the communications with his lawyer. I did this and the lawyer said he was working on the case but these family matters always took a long time to resolve.

Later, in fact months later, I received another call from the man. He said his lawyer had sent him a summons to appear in court in San Juan to answer charges of child abuse. He said he was now scared as well as angry. Scared that he would never see his children again and angry that such charges had been so obviously fabricated. I again could not comment. He then sent me a large folder with all sorts of character references including one from the Attorney General of the Cayman Islands. Again, all I could do was to pass this on to his lawyer. It was now just over a year since I first became involved in the case.

The Attorney General's letter included references to the international convention on child abduction and how that document related to Puerto Rico and the Cayman Islands. The convention was between sovereign nations and since both Puerto Rico and the Cayman Islands were territories of sovereign nations the legal ramifications were murky. Again, I could only refer this to the lawyer.

The court hearing was postponed many times and it was well into the second year of my involvement before the case was finally heard. Predictably, the local court awarded full custody to the wife and very limited visiting rights to the father. The man returned to the Cayman Islands and more time passed.

The man called me again when, according to him, he had tried several times to visit his children but was denied all access by his wife's family. The fact that he had traveled from the Cayman Islands to visit them at a previously agreed date seemed to be of no consequence. He claimed that he was also denied access to them by telephone. Again, I said, there was nothing I could do directly since it was up to his lawyer to pursue the issue with the courts. He said the Cayman Islands Attorney General would be writing to the Puerto Rican Secretary of Justice complaining about the treatment and non-compliance with the court-established visiting rights.

Months later—we were now into year three—he called again to say that the Puerto Rican Secretary of Justice had not replied to the Attorney General's letter and could I intervene. I checked with my own bosses and requested a meeting with the Secretary of Justice. In that meeting I described the facts as I knew them and they said they would investigate the case thoroughly and let me know. More months passed.

Eventually, the Office of the Secretary told me that the case was closed. The court was satisfied that the father was a child abuser and they had cut visiting rights completely. They further reported that, given that situation, there was nothing the Department of Justice could do since it was the jurisdiction of the courts to decide such matters. They said the decision would have to be appealed through the proper channels. Four years of effort and the case had gone inexorably downhill. I informed the father and the Cayman Islands' Attorney General.

And there, as far as I know, the case still sits. It is immensely sad and, although one should not get emotionally involved in such things, it is difficult not to. Whatever the real story is, the man will probably not see his children until they are adults and able to make decisions for themselves. Even then, it may not happen. Very sad.

TRIBUTE TO DIANA

"his staff had petitioned him to ask me… It was humbling."

There are many heart-wrenching stories related to the death of Princess Diana, and they occurred in many countries. The tragedy touched the world in way that had not been experienced since the death of President Kennedy or, more recently, the events of September 11, 2001 in New York City. However, the emotional reaction to the Princess's death brought a level of international unity that is probably unique.

The reaction in Puerto Rico was no less than that of any other community and so I offer the following as a tribute to our collective grief and to that of Puerto Ricans specifically.

The local reaction to the tragedy certainly occupied the office for many days. Equally, I am sure that British consulates around the world all experienced heartfelt outpourings of grief and in no way would I suggest that Puerto Rico's reactions were unique. However, they were overwhelming and poignant.

One of the most surprising reactions was when I arrived at my office to find garlands of flowers taped to the flagpole. I should add that the consulate was located in a regular office building with many other businesses, yet the Union Jack outside proved to be a magnet for expressions of grief. There were flowers continually taped to the pole for over a month.

People came from all over the island to sign the books of condolence. I particularly remember one elderly lady who came, on public transportation, from Utuado, a small town in the middle of the mountains. The journey must have taken her at least all day.

The Puerto Rican Legislature passed resolutions of sympathy and the President of the Senate asked if he could come to my office to present the formal document. They were even kind enough to prepare a formal copy for me to keep. It remains a treasured possession.

To put the whole Puerto Rican reaction in perspective, I will recount an incident that happened about three weeks after the Princess died. I was in Arecibo, a regional centre on the north central coast of the island where, for many years, I had acted as a consultant in my professional capacity (remember, honorary consuls are not paid.)

There was a small *panaderia* called Coffee Break on the main plaza where I always bought coffee and the occasional illicit (from my diet's point of view) cinnamon roll. Apart from "*Buenos Dias, como estas,*" the staff of Coffee Break and I had never really conversed. They probably knew I was a consultant for the Municipality but knew nothing about me beyond that—they had no reason to be interested.

On this morning I went in to buy my non-fattening roll and coffee and the owner asked, rather timidly, if he could talk to me for a minute. To my amazement he said that all of his staff wished to sign the condolence book if that was possible. Why he would have known that I was the British Consul I have no idea. It had nothing to do with my work in Arecibo.

He said that his staff had petitioned him to ask me. The following week I took one of the books of condolence with me and they all signed it individually. They also, to a person, wrote a short message thanking me profusely for permitting them to express their feelings. It was humbling.

BACK TO JAIL

I've put this short story in the "Heart-Wrenching" category because, despite the obvious guilt involved, I feel a little sad about the circumstances of the person's return to jail. Some cases just affect you that way.

One of the delights of holding consular positions is that you are obliged to visit British citizens in jail. The requirement states that such visits should take place at least once every six months. Television occasionally covers high profile cases around the world but prison visits happen on a regular basis in all locations.

What is slightly disconcerting is that these visits take place, at least in the penitentiary in San Juan, in small rooms with no prison officers present. The first time that happened to me, I was meeting a man who had been jailed for multiple murders.

I had received a request from the U.S. federal authorities at the penitentiary in San Juan to issue an emergency passport for a British inmate who was to be extradited back to the U.K. I had not previously known that he was in jail but such situations were fairly normal if the inmate did not actually request consular visits. In order to issue an emergency passport I had to interview the person to determine, to the best of my knowledge, that he was in fact British. I should explain that emergency passports are only issued to get the recipient back to their home country. These passports can be used only once and are issued to cover the timeframe of the repatriation.

The interview began with the person telling me that he had been arrested in the U.K. for drug smuggling fifteen years previously. He said he had served five years of his seven year sentence and then, during a weekend parole, had simply disappeared. He made his way to the Caribbean and had spent the last ten years as a charter boat captain operating mainly out of St. Thomas in the U.S. Virgin Islands. (I had thought all British jailbirds, or potential jailbirds, went to Marbella in Spain, or maybe that's only the rich ones!)

He said that, after a few years as a charter captain, he had obtained a British passport on the island of St. Martin using a false name. How he managed to do that he did not explain, which was probably just as well. If I had known I would have had to report it and that would have created a mountain of paperwork and volumes of phone calls.

Two years previous to our meeting, his boat had hit something in open ocean at night and sank with all his documents on board. Such events are unfortunately all too common in the Caribbean, where there are so many yachts and so much commercial traffic. You really would not believe how many containers fall off ships and float just under the surface. One of those could sink a speeding frigate, let alone a fiberglass sailboat!

He said he filed an insurance claim, bought a new boat, and, a year later, received a warrant for his arrest from Interpol, the European police agency. Somehow his insurance claim had triggered a computer inquiry and Interpol identified him as an escaped parolee. It's good to know the system does work occasionally!

He was duly arrested, much to the amazement of his new wife who knew nothing of his incarceration in England or even his real name. The authorities in St. Thomas, who arrested him on behalf of Interpol, then transported him to the federal penitentiary in San Juan, pending his extradition back to the U.K.

He calmly concluded that his new boat was in his wife's name and that he expected to serve out his two remaining years in the U.K., plus a few months, and then return to his life in the Caribbean, finally free of his past. The following day he departed under guard for London.

The meeting in the penitentiary was our only contact but it somehow struck a cord with me. I often wonder whether his wife and seven-month-old child were waiting for him when he returned. I hope so!

CHAPTER X
SERIOUS

NORMAL CONSULAR WORK

"Can you tell me what were the burial rites practiced in England in medieval times and before?"

All of the other chapters entitled "Serious" describe specific situations or incidents. This one will attempt to give a flavor of the normal and regular consular work.

It would be a travesty to portray what happened on a daily basis as always being bizarre, funny, or amazing. Most of the time it was routine assistance to British subjects and promotion of British trade and investment. This may not be quite so amusing to read as some of the other stories, but it is a major part of the picture nonetheless; different, and a counterpoint perhaps.

Many honorary consuls do not exactly start work at the crack of dawn although many of them start before their paid brethren in full consular posts. One such paid, or career, consul in San Juan opened his office at ten thirty every day and closed it at noon. He played golf every afternoon and received a full salary as far as I know. (I will admit to being horrified and wildly jealous at the same time. He lived in the same building as me and represented the other country in the Falklands War. Since I was on a higher floor, I was tempted to hang the U.K. flag out of the window. We honorary consuls must have our small pleasures, if only mentally.)

The following events all happened at the times I've given but they didn't all happen on the same day. I've just put it together that way to give a flavor of the work.

7:30 A.M.:

I am met at the office door by three crew-members of a cruise ship who want their British passports renewed. Their ship is only in port one day, once a week, so it has to be done during that time. I explain the forms, tell them where they can get passport photographs (but not until the shop opens at 9 A.M., and let them know the cost (no cash or checks but money orders). They leave to get the photos and the money.

8:15 A.M.:

Phone call: "Can you tell me what detailed effect the 'Magna Carta' had on the British monarchy and the development of the parliamentary system?" (At 8:15 in the morning, they have to be kidding!) I answer as best I can but with the strong advice that they should seek a more knowledgeable source.

9:00 A.M.:

Call British Embassy in Washington to get dispensation for the cruise ship staff and their passport requests. I will have to send the documents to Washington for them, I need them turned around in a week, and they will have to be sent back to me. Washington is getting used to this request and complies.

9:45 A.M.:

Meeting with the Puerto Rican Secretary of Justice about an international child abduction protocol and its relevance to a case involving the Cayman Islands (remember that story?). I have to wait for forty-five minutes beyond the appointed time before I am seen—quite normal, I might add, if a total waste of time. I still feel better arriving on time knowing that I will have to wait at least thirty minutes, even after thirty years of Puerto Rican training—cultures die hard.

11:30 A.M.:

Back at the office. Call five major British companies to request appointments for a British Deputy Consul General who will be visiting the island in six months time. This is a perfect clash of cultures. If you make appointments in Puerto Rico further ahead than three weeks before the required date, no one takes you seriously and they forget. British government officials, however, want their calendars completed six months before the actual date. And I'm in the middle!

The other problem with this is that the official only wants to arrange the visits so he can write them up in his visit report. He has nothing of any value to say and we all know it. So I have to say to the companies, "You know this is a waste of time as much as I do but I have no choice." They actually appreciate the honesty— they have similar problems with their bosses.

12:30 P.M.:

Consular Corps lunch in a local restaurant. I arrive at 12:50 P.M. I am the second one there. We sit down at 1:45 P.M. and listen to various accolades for our own membership followed by the giving of plaques. (Consular Corps are big on giving themselves as many decorations as possible. The fact that some of them look as though they were purchased in K-Mart is irrelevant. I leave before the dessert and coffee.)

3:00 P.M.:

Visit to one of the local hospitals. A British subject, who was badly injured on a sailing ship and evacuated to San Juan in a U.S. Navy helicopter, doesn't speak Spanish and the nurses don't speak English. He has no shoes, toothpaste, or anything else. I call my wife. She gathers what she can from home when she returns from work and we go back in the evening to give him something.

4:00 P.M.:

Back at the office. Phone call from a mother. My child has a school project. Can I tell her what is our national costume (we don't have one), our national anthem (she wants me to sing it so she can understand the rhythm!), our national flower (rose, I think, but that is England, which means the Scots, Welsh and Irish will kill me if they find out) and, finally, do we have any posters I can send by mail (no). She thanks me.

4:15 P.M.:

A lady calls to complain that the planes flying overhead and the electrical wires on poles close to her house are giving her cancer (what have I done to deserve this, I wonder). You can't really say what you actually think so you have to slowly work your way out of the problem. Tomorrow's headline: "British Consul tells elderly lady she is a moron"—you never know who their relatives might be.)

4:30 P.M.:

Phone call: "Can you tell me how many provinces there are in China?"

"Excuse me," I reply, "why are you calling the British Consulate?"

"Well! China belongs to England."

Of course, doesn't everyone know that!

I should add that during my tenure I had that question innumerable times not only relating to China, but Saudi Arabia, Belgium, and many others. I know we used to own a third of the world but things have changed a little!

4:45 P.M.:

Visit of a British couple who have lost all their possessions in a robbery. They are tourists and the wife put her bag down for two minutes and it was gone. All their money, credit cards, air tickets, and passports gone. I call their daughter in England and they explain. She promises to send an electronic ticket the following day. I issue them emergency passports to get them home and they leave. They have one night left on their pre-paid hotel. It's now 6:15 P.M. and I was supposed to pick my wife up fifteen minutes ago for a reception on a visiting French Navy ship which starts at 6:30 P.M. The phone rings and I, like an idiot, pick it up.

6:15 P.M.:

"Can you tell me what were the burial rites practiced in England in medieval times and before? I am an officer in the Puerto Rican National Guard and I have a major project to finish tonight." I almost ask the obvious question but restrain myself, I don't really want to know and I'm too tired. I answer as best I can and he seems happy.

We arrive at the ship an hour late and are still ahead of most of the local invitees!

In between all this I am supposed to be earning a living from my own company!

CHAPTER XI
AMAZING

This chapter contains stories and experiences that amazed me when they happened. In retrospect, they still amaze me and, in doing so, enter the realm of fond memories.

The lady who called asking for "The Wedding Cake" recipe was quite sincere and probably thought I knew the answer. Why else would she have called?

The "Cake Maker's Yacht" was so obviously an insurance scam that I have to wonder if there was not a great deal more to the story. No one in their right mind would have paid out based on the stated circumstances.

"One Almost-Dead Motorcycle Escort" is probably an everyday occurrence. It is just that it happened to me in rather auspicious circumstances, which made it memorable and funny.

"Marie Celeste—1990s Style" mirrors the mystery of the original story while, unlike that story, eventually providing a plausible, though amazing, explanation. The vagaries of the sea remain unpredictable.

Finally, "The Gentleman's Club" produced disbelief in almost everyone it touched. The Consulate General in New York didn't believe me at first and I'm not sure I was fully convinced of what I was promoting either.

THE WEDDING CAKE

"Could I give her the recipe, please?"

Consuls are fountains of all knowledge. Everyone knows that. The only exceptions to this global perception are the consuls themselves and maybe their families. They are regularly asked the most amazing questions in the apparent absolute belief that the correct answer is certain to be forthcoming. A case in point is the following story.

A lady called and informed me that her daughter was getting married in six months' time. She had a question, the answer to which would not only make the wedding a complete success but would also fulfill a mother's promise.

(Stop for a minute and try to imagine the thoughts that might run through your head as you sit there waiting for the punch-line. To use an old English expression, the mind boggles.)

Somewhat disappointingly perhaps, the lady went on to explain that the mother's promise was a wedding cake made to the same recipe as that of Princess Diana's wedding cake. She said she had searched high and low for the recipe when someone said, "The British consul will know." Obviously one of those who thought consuls know everything.

Could I give her the recipe, please?

After a while you get used to this sort of request—amazing requests I mean, not the request for the recipe—and you take them in your stride. It was always tempting to make something up since the chance they would ever know the difference was minimal. However, integrity intervened, or maybe it was the thought of being sued for killing people with my recipe.

I vaguely remembered (my usual state, since I was supposed to be over sixty-five, white-haired, and blessed with a stick!) that

Princess Diana's cake had been made by the Royal Air Force. I have absolutely no idea why—either why I remembered or why the RAF made it—so I suggested the lady call the RAF liaison officer in the Washington Embassy (they don't have any planes to play with in Washington so I was doing him a favor by giving him something useful to do!)

All in a day's work at the honorary consulate!

THE CAKE MAKER'S YACHT

"If you were the insurance adjuster, would you believe that story?"

The U.S. Coast Guard called me at home early one morning. They informed me that a luxury yacht had sent out a "mayday" call just off the north coast of Puerto Rico and had then sunk. They thought the yacht was registered to a British subject but they were not altogether sure. They further told me that the crew had been rescued, several of whom were British citizens, and they were en-route to San Juan courtesy of the Coast Guard cutter that had rescued them. The officer said he would keep me posted of their arrival time and where the crew would be staying. This was a fairly routine call apart, obviously, from the loss of the yacht. Nobody appeared to have been hurt and the procedures for repatriating the crew seemed straightforward. It was only after interviewing the captain and the crew that the essence of this story became clear.

The yacht had apparently left St. Thomas in the U.S. Virgin Islands heading towards Florida late the previous evening; St. Thomas is about sixty miles east of Puerto Rico. Sometime early in the following morning the crew-member on watch noticed that the yacht appeared to be slowing down for no apparent reason. She called the captain.

Now I should also mention that the yacht was well over a

hundred feet in length and had a crew of, I believe, nine. One would think that, on a yacht that size, either there would be an engine room watch as well as a bridge watch or the engine room would be so electronically "wired" that the bridge watch would know exactly what was going on down there every minute of the day. There was no engine room watch and the person on bridge watch only noticed that the yacht appeared to be slowing down (this was my first alarm bell if you will excuse the pun.)

The captain said he went down to the engine room to check and discovered that the engines were almost entirely under water. *The engines were under water and there were NO ALARMS!*—my second alarm bell. He decided that it was too late to save the yacht and sounded the abandon ship klaxon—at least that one worked, apparently. He sent out a "mayday" call and climbed into the yacht's dinghy with the other crew members. The yacht, he said, "sank within a few minutes."

Now, presumably, all the other crew-members had been sleeping while this was going on—it was three o'clock in the morning. The yacht sank within a few minutes of the captain sounding the "abandon ship" alarm and they all nonchalantly climbed into the dingy and sat there awaiting rescue. Oh, and they all just happened to have their passports and other important documents with them in waterproof bags. In all honesty I am told that this is standard procedure on such boats for the captain to retain all such documents in this manner but it did seem just a touch convenient.

The "mayday" call was answered first by a Royal Navy frigate, which came steaming over the horizon at a high rate of knots, and picked them up. There is normally only one Royal Navy frigate in the whole Caribbean at any one time so the coincidence of this rescue is rather extraordinary. The U.S. Coast Guard then appeared on the scene and the rescued crew-members were transferred to the Coast Guard cutter for the trip to San Juan. The frigate, I presume, continued on its patrol.

The cutter brought the crew to San Juan and put them in a small hotel where I met them a few hours later. They all appeared to be in fine shape, had called their relatives and were ready to fly out, first-class no less, back to the U.K. that afternoon.

They had just let a multi-million dollar yacht sink and the owner was paying for them to fly home first-class. He must have been extremely forgiving!

It gets worse.

After a little probing the captain admitted that a slight leak in a seawater valve had been reported in the engine room before the yacht left St. Thomas (another alarm bell for me). Who in their right mind sets off on a thousand-mile voyage with a known seawater leak in the engine room? If you were the insurance adjuster, would you believe that story? Oh! I almost forgot, the yacht just happened to sink right over the Puerto Rican Trench, which is five miles straight down. The chances, therefore, of finding any evidence was nil. I was never contacted by any authorities after the event nor by any insurance company. I can only assume they paid up or it was written off as a business deduction! However, my curiosity eventually got the better of me and I tried to track down the owner of the yacht. The reply came back that it was a millionaire (surprise, surprise) who had made his fortune baking cakes.

One more for the memoirs!

ONE ALMOST-DEAD MOTORCYCLE ESCORT

"He was playing to rule number three; all official vehicles following are the same width as a motorcycle."

Anyone who has ever been involved in dealing with motorcycle escorts can relate to this story. I'm sure it happens frequently but it's still funny (afterwards).

Motorcycle escorts, I have come to believe, operate under a fixed set of rules. The problem is they never tell anyone else what those rules are.

Well, the first rule of the game is that motorcycle escorts are completely exempt from all rules of the road. The second rule of the game is that anyone who has the audacity to be on the road at the same time as the motorcycles should be treated with the disdain and belligerence they deserve for such presumptuous behavior. The third rule of the game is that all vehicles, and particularly those in the official party being escorted, are the same width as one motorcycle.

Now, with the ground rules clear, I can begin the story.

A visit by a member of the British royal family to San Juan, even an unofficial visit, always prompted a flurry of diplomatic and security activity and this was no exception. Protocol officials had to decide which vehicles should be used and who should ride in them. They also had to decide orders of precedence in the receiving lines and myriad details that sometimes seem slightly ridiculous. Sometimes!

In this particular case it was decided that I should drive the lead car in the procession from the airport with the royal visitor in the car behind and innumerable other cars and police cruisers behind that. However, there were to be two motorcycle outriders in front of me to act rather like a bow wave in clearing passage through the unfortunate mortals who happened to be on the road at the same time.

I didn't realize at first that the two riders actually had two separate jobs. One was assigned to stay just in front of me and yell at all the traffic we passed. The other was assigned to ride ahead like a maniac to the next road junction, stop, and block all cross traffic regardless of any minor impediments like traffic lights, main roads, stop signs, or anything else for that matter.

One result of this type of behavior is that the general motoring public tends to become seriously upset. They take the only route left to them which is to sit still, get mad, and blow their horns. So, not only did we have a motorcade that was traveling too fast for its own good, we had maniacal motorcycle outriders with sirens blaring and traffic all around blowing their horns. It made for quite a peaceful, relaxing, and certainly low profile arrival! Any security threat could have pinpointed their target from the noise alone.

I quickly got used to the two motorcycles playing leapfrog, although it proved quite difficult to keep up with the one who was weaving through traffic ahead of me. He was playing to rule number three; all official vehicles following are the same width as a motorcycle.

After a mile or so of this chase I have to admit to a sneaking smile—this was fun! I was getting quite good at it and was beginning to realize that all official vehicles really do shrink to the width of motorcycles. Suddenly the outriders instituted rule number four, which no one had told me about. That's the rule that says they switch roles after every ten road junctions. The one that had been leading me came to a screeching halt to stop some cross traffic. How I missed him I have absolutely no idea, but miss him I did and I just kept going. A few minutes later, he whistled past me bound for the next road junction, his partner became my leader and so we continued on into town.

They didn't seem the slightest bit phased by the fact that one of them nearly died, but my car had suddenly grown back to its normal width.

MARIE CELESTE—1990S STYLE

"The yacht was found by HMS London *six months later after drifting for 2700 miles in the North Atlantic."*

The Roosevelt Roads Base, on the eastern shore of Puerto Rico, was one of the U.S. Navy's major training facilities. It is the only base in the world where they can practice full carrier fleet exercises. I say "was" because it closed shortly before this book was published. Interestingly Roosevelt Road was originally built to house the British Home Fleet if Hitler had invaded Britain in World War II. So the Royal Navy's connection to the base is illustrious and long. A bunker was even prepared for the King and the royal family!

This story begins with a call from the Port Control officer for the base. He said that a crew of Royal Navy officers and ratings were attempting to enter the base in a thirty-five foot sailboat. That, in itself, did not sound too amazing but the sailboat was accompanied by a Royal Navy frigate. That was a little unusual. The Port Officer said that the Royal Navy wanted to turn the sailboat over to the U.S. Navy. Definitely unusual!

I promised to talk to the captain of *HMS London*, the frigate involved, and find out what this was all about. The Port Officer made it quite clear that his commanding officer was not about to take responsibility for the yacht (why they needed me in the middle of this I have no idea—don't they have radios that can talk to each other? We are supposed to be allies after all).

I managed to get patched through to the frigate and asked the skipper what this was all about. He explained that they were crossing the Atlantic on patrol when they spotted a twin-mast ketch, apparently drifting, about two hundred miles south of Bermuda. The yacht had no sails up but appeared to be in good order. However, there was no sign of any crew or any rapid evacuation. A typical *Marie Celeste* story.

The Captain decided to put a prize crew on board and sail it ahead of the frigate straight south about eight hundred miles to the Roosevelt Roads Navy Base where the frigate was due a week later. The frigate and yacht both arrived off Puerto Rico about the same time and entered the base together. One is tempted to wonder why we switched from sail to steam, or gas turbine, if it was just as fast, but I digress. The captain wanted to turn over responsibility for the yacht to the U.S. Navy and retrieve his crew. Unfortunately the U.S. Navy rather ruined those plans by refusing to assume responsibility.

The Captain was now rather stuck and was grateful for any

advice I could offer. I assumed he had told his superiors who, more than likely, said something to the effect of, "You got yourself into this mess so you can get yourself out of it."

I suggested that he take the yacht to the British Virgin Islands, and leave it there with the governor. It was a relatively short distance and it was a British jurisdiction. I understand that it is what he finally did but it's the rest of the story that's amazing. Where did the yacht come from in the first place?

It took several months of investigation before the full story came out. The yacht had originally left Germany to sail across the Atlantic to the Caribbean. (As an aside, it always amazes me how many people do this on quite small yachts. One of the British people who was posted to Puerto Rico to head a major corporation let his wife and his two children, both under fourteen, sail his forty-two foot ketch from the U.K. to Puerto Rico. Haven't these people heard the ocean is dangerous?)

Anyway, the German crew of the yacht reached the Canary Islands safely; the Canary Islands have been the jump-off point for sailing west to the Caribbean since Columbus's day. They decided to spend a few days ashore and so moored the yacht to a buoy in the harbor and found a hotel. Two days later, when they returned, the yacht wasn't there. After reporting it lost, and probably stolen, they began a search but failed to find any trace. They eventually gave up and went back home to claim the loss on their insurance. It had obviously been stolen, or perhaps sunk. The harbor itself was quite deep and the immediate offshore depths were impressive. End of story as far as they were concerned.

The part I find amazing is that the time lapse between the date their yacht disappeared and the date *HMS London* found it drifting was a little over six months. How the yacht survived in good shape while drifting over twenty-seven hundred miles in the north Atlantic in winter defies belief.

It must have just slipped its moorings and drifted away happily on its own. It definitely had a Marie Celeste disposition!

The Gentleman's Club

"They gave me a life membership to the new club."

Over a period of several years I had heard many reports from various visiting British businessmen about a certain "Gentleman's Club" in the tourist district of San Juan. I knew where it was since it was on one of the main tourist streets. (I, of course, had never been inside.)

I had been frequently told it was a "high class" gentleman's club, whatever that might mean. Such clubs exist in all major cities and attract much of their clientele from the ranks of "visiting firemen"—accompanying those visiting firemen is also the excuse locals use for frequenting the club themselves.

I was sitting at my desk one day, minding my own business, when I received a call about setting up businesses in the United Kingdom and a request for an appointment to discuss the procedures involved. This was fairly unusual from a jurisdiction like Puerto Rico, but since it represented inward investment to the U.K., I was naturally interested.

One of the main jobs of British consulates overseas is to attract as much foreign investment into the U.K. as possible. Opportunities to do this do not arise very often in an honorary consulate, particularly one in Puerto Rico, so I immediately set up the meeting.

On the appointed hour a couple arrived and introduced themselves as the owners and operators of the aforementioned gentleman's club. To say I was slightly taken aback would be putting it mildly. However, you do learn to keep a straight face in this job and to react quickly. My reaction, by the way, had nothing to do with being prudish, it came more from the mental picture of trying to explain to the bureaucrats in the British government the importance of this particular investment. I could just imagine their faces and their comments. (The overwhelming need to at least smile at such thoughts was quite a distraction, but we diplomats are made of strong stuff!)

The British government has a set of regulations and requirements for those wishing to establish businesses in the United Kingdom. I located the correct forms and offered to help in any way I could. I also said I would check with my head office in New York to establish the exact procedures necessary.

The couple seemed perfectly serious. They knew where they wanted to establish their club and they had visited the site in southern England several times. They left with the appropriate paperwork and with a promise to avail themselves of my help in the near future. It crossed my mind to offer to meet them in their offices next time, all in the name of British government service of course, but I restrained myself.

My next stop was to present this unique investment opportunity to the Consulate General in New York. I dragged that discussion out for as long as I could without actually telling them the nature of the business. Cruel, maybe, but I couldn't resist. When the New York official eventually discovered what the business involved, my reputation changed levels by several points. Whether it was up or down I'm not sure but I could take a shrewd guess. (I always felt, throughout my time as honorary consul, a certain obligation to tease a little humor out of the bureaucracy. It didn't work most of the time but there were occasional flashes of hope.)

Several months passed in the exchange of paperwork and the fulfillment of requirements. All required steps were rigorously followed and the application for the establishment of a gentleman's club in Bournemouth was approved. I could tell that certain people in the government were not too happy about the approval, and I'm sure they did not list it on their reports of successful inward investments, but approve it they did.

The couple duly departed for the U.K. and their new venture.

Some time afterwards I asked my brother, who lives in the area, if he had heard anything about such a club. He not only had heard all about it, it was prominently featured in the local newspaper and there were ads for it all over town. He also filled me in on all the gossip that surrounded the club's opening.

I'm glad they successfully made the transition from Puerto Rico to Bournemouth. Not just because of all the hard work they put into the process or even because the whole idea appealed to my irreverent sense of humor but because, before they left, they gave me a life membership to the new club! I'm still debating whether to tell my brother!

CHAPTER XII
SERIOUS

THE JAGUAR DEALERSHIP

"I wrote a letter to the head of Jaguar North America that is still the closest I have knowingly come to asking for a libel suit."

The establishment of the official Jaguar dealership in Puerto Rico was an excellent example of what pure persistence can achieve. It is also a documentary on the challenge facing individuals trying to deal with large corporations. It was extremely frustrating but, ultimately, extremely successful. And it only took about five years of my time!

When I began working as Honorary Consul, I looked for flagship products and companies that would announce the presence of British interest in Puerto Rico just by their very existence; names like Jaguar, ICI, and Lloyds are recognized worldwide.

ICI did establish a major pharmaceutical operation on the island during my tenure but I would be presumptuous to claim I had anything more than a peripheral hand in that initiative. Jaguar, on the other hand, was a different story.

Puerto Rico has a Mr. Jaguar. He sold Jaguars to those who wanted them and offered full service. He mostly imported the cars from the U.S. mainland and had built a good relationship with some of the dealers there for parts and even warranty services. However, he had been singularly unsuccessful in acquiring a formal dealership. He had been trying for over five years. I needed a flagship name and he wanted the dealership. It sounded like a profitable joint venture.

Honorary consuls do not normally get involved in such mundane issues as trade. Historically, that has not been why they were appointed. However, I thought it was important from an image point of view and so I followed my conviction. At the time it didn't win me many friends in the British Government hierarchy—trade was below their dignity in many cases. Today, trade is considered one of the main reasons for the appointments of new honorary consuls. Was I responsible? Unlikely, although it would be nice to think I contributed.

The first job was to find out who, within the Jaguar corporate structure, had responsibility for Puerto Rico. Jaguar North America Inc. had the island specified in their contract but wasn't interested in developing the market. I tried several approaches, even using the weight of the main consular offices in New York, but was met with polite indifference at best. The one response I did get merely indicated that Puerto Rico was an insignificant market and thus fell below the corporate horizon. They obviously had no idea of the potential that existed. The fact that there were already three hundred Jaguars on the island did not seem to interest them—a dead end!

The next step was to go straight to the factory in England. I had a trip planned anyway and managed to persuade someone in Coventry to see me (my job title does have its uses at times). We met at the Brown's Lane facilities and they were very polite but also had no idea of the potential or even where the island was located. However, in the end they did agree to look into the matter and to see if cars could be shipped direct.

After several months, and several encouraging conversations, they said their contract with Jaguar North America included all U.S. specification cars and that covered Puerto Rico. They said they did not consider areas like Puerto Rico when they signed their North American contract and now they were stuck with that legal restriction. First full circle of the bureaucratic merry-go-round!

(This was not the first time I encountered that particular problem. British companies often signed U.S. distribution contracts without considering offshore jurisdictions like Puerto Rico. It was a serious problem in encouraging British imports and, in many cases, remains a problem. U.S. distributors, in general, know less about the island than people in the U.K. and often don't care.)

The factory in Coventry did make inquiries with Jaguar North America about separating Puerto Rico from their contract. They were told in no uncertain terms to mind their own business. The factory explained that Jaguar North America was by far their largest market and they were not about to fight with their main sales agent. Understandable but frustrating! This marked the first anniversary of my involvement in the project. Why was Jaguar so important and what was the real potential?

Puerto Rico, at that point, had Mercedes sales approaching three hundred a year, Volvo sales of just over a thousand a year and a total vehicle population of almost a million. The Island boasted the highest per capita income in the whole of Latin America and the Caribbean. They could afford Jaguars and they wanted them. They certainly had a taste for luxury cars. I found it totally amazing, for example, that in that same year, people on the Island had bought ten Maserati Quattroports when the entire factory production of that luxury model was one hundred a year. There was a market for Jaguars but no one in Jaguar was interested.

The only way forward was to keep up the pressure on both fronts. Push the factory and be a general nuisance to Jaguar North America. Jaguar North America eventually reacted by formally stating that they were not interested in markets that only had the potential for thirty new cars a year. Where that figure came from we had absolutely no idea. It was probably fabricated to make us go away. Bloody-mindedness began to influence my determination.

Then we got a lucky break. In one of its regular reorganizations the factory bought out Jaguar North America Inc. Where they got the money I have no idea since most of the reorganizations during that era were designed to avoid bankruptcy. (Corporate finance still mystifies me since it seems to be normal practice to borrow large sums just before declaring bankruptcy. Gives you great confidence in the vision of your bankers!)

We allowed time for the factory to absorb its new acquisi-tion—these things always take quite a few months and in between, no employee will dare make a decision since everyone's job is in question. (We were now approaching three years from the start of my involvement and eight from the beginning of the local Jaguar man's involvement.)

Continual harassment of the factory and the North American staff finally produced a visit to the island from the New Jersey based marketing staff. The marketing manager went away convinced, or so he said, that the Puerto Rican market deserved serious attention. That sounded like a different kind of brush-off but at least the door had been opened a crack. Several more visits followed and a constant stream of information was exchanged. Progress at last, hopefully.

Just over four years from the start of this saga, we received news that a team from Jaguar was to visit Puerto Rico to interview and research all possible candidates for a formal dealership. Success at last! The team came, did its job, and returned to New Jersey. I then received a call telling me that they had decided to award the dealership to the Mercedes dealer. I couldn't believe my ears. After all that work they were stupid enough to give the dealership to the one person who had most to lose from it; namely, his Mercedes sales. The two brands competed head-to-head. Of course he wanted it. He wanted to make sure it never competed with his main business and there was no better way than to control it and quietly kill it. There are many examples of this happening in the car business and they should have recog-nized the situation. Rank idiocy—perhaps I should have put this story under the Chapter heading "Just Plain Stupid".

I decided I had stuck my neck so far that I should go for broke. I wrote a letter to the head of Jaguar North America that still is the closest I have ever knowingly come to asking for a libel suit. It basically suggested that a decision as stupid as that had to have extenuating circumstances. I didn't quite say the decision had been bought and sold but I came extremely close. There really was no other logical explanation.

I waited. Whether for a change of heart or a lawsuit, I wasn't quite sure.

Finally the news came that the existing, unofficial, Jaguar dealer should prepare a full proposal for the dealership. It worked! Victory at last.

Many months and much paperwork later the President of Jaguar North America came to Puerto Rico to open the new Jaguar dealership. Five years from my starting point and ten from the dealer's first inquiries—definitely champagne time!

The dealership sold seventy cars the first year and currently sells in the region of three hundred. This, despite a local import tax on all vehicles that places a full-size Jaguar in the $80,000 range. Vindication!

I should have negotiated for five or ten per cent of the business instead of agreeing to a demonstration car being assigned to me on a rotating basis, which never actually happened.

Hindsight is wonderful!

CHAPTER XIII
JUST PLAIN STUPID

I almost titled this section "I wonder how they survived into adulthood." The things people do are truly amazing or, in many cases, just plain stupid.

"Deportation is Fun" concerns someone who kept repeating the same mistake. Not only is that nonsensical in a general situation, when it involves the violation of a deportation order it is downright idiotic and dangerous. Yet he did not seem particularly concerned that he would be spending time in jail. I shall leave the readers to judge his continuing ability to survive.

"Pimm's and Slaves" really annoyed me when it happened. On reflection, it still really annoys me. How a major trading company can be so short-sighted and arrogant and yet survive for three hundred years is totally beyond me. Unfortunately, it's not a unique case. The title might suggest there is a link between Pimm's and slaves. That, to my knowledge, is definitely not the case. The relationship is between the distribution company involved and slaves, although even that is conjecture on my part. Difficult to refute perhaps, but conjecture nonetheless!

"Deportation is Fun—Part Two" should teach us all to be very careful when dealing with immigration issues. It shows that it is not always advisable to believe what you are told the first time—even if those telling you should be the authority on the subject. You don't mess around with Immigration—ever, for any reason. They seem to be one of the few government agencies of any country that can, almost literally, put you in jail and throw the key away!

DEPORTATION IS FUN!

"And you wonder where your tax money goes!"

Deportation *must* be fun, or else the person in this story should be condemned under the title of this chapter.

I received a call from the Governor's Office in the British Virgin Islands. Apparently a young woman had come to the office to complain that her boyfriend had been arrested in St. Thomas in the U.S. Virgin Islands. She said he had subsequently been shipped to the Federal Penitentiary in San Juan to await trial on an immigration violation.

I called my normal contact in the U.S. Federal Penitentiary and inquired when I might see this person. An appointment was arranged and I listened to his story. He started by telling me how much he loved his girlfriend and requested that I please tell her and make arrangements for her to call him. I had to report back to the Governor's Office in Road Town, Tortola, anyway so I said I would pass on his message. He then began his story and it is here that the "just plain stupid" part begins.

About ten years before, he had visited the U.S., overstayed his visa deadline, and was eventually caught and deported. By U.S. law, if deportation takes place, a person cannot return to the U.S. under any circumstances for five years and then, for five years after that, special permission is required.

He decided to enter the U.S. again, only this time through Canada. He was caught at the border by U.S. Immigration and held on violation of deportation charges. The Canadians certainly didn't want him back so he was summarily returned to the U.K.

Three years later he decided to take his girlfriend on holiday to the British Virgin Islands. After a few days on the beach he thought it would be a nice idea to rent a boat to tour the smaller islands in the area. However, the only boats available were in the U.S. Virgin Islands—U.S. territory! He jumped on the ferry for the half-hour run to Redhook in St. Thomas, landed, and was immediately arrested for a second attempted violation of deportation regulations. There are no detention facilities in St. Thomas so he was sent to the nearest Federal prison, which is in San Juan.

(Quite honestly, he should have been arrested for arrant stupidity but I suppose there is no statute against that.)

When I met him he had been in the San Juan prison for a month. I reported the situation back to the Governor in Tortola who told me the man's girlfriend had returned to England. However, she had left behind a large bag with the man's personal effects. The Governor wanted to send them to me so I could return them. (And you wonder where your tax money goes!)

Naturally, the contents of the bag had to be inventoried and they proved to be pictures of the girlfriend in various poses of total undress.

I often wonder what the Foreign Office auditors did with that file when they found it in the Governor's archives—leaked it to the tabloids probably!

I, of course, merely reviewed the inventory list without looking at the pictures, made a copy (of the inventory list!), and passed it all on to the U.S. authorities in the penitentiary. They, I assume, passed them onto the man.

He was eventually charged and, after several months in jail, was permitted to pay his own way back to the U.K. I'm a little surprised they didn't just throw the key away but then it's very expensive to keep someone in a penitentiary. Fortunately he did not appear again during my tenure although it would not have surprised me.

Pimm's & Slaves

"…I didn't have to worry about being diplomatic, and they needed the wakeup call."

This story goes back to the beginning of my work as Honorary Consul. In fact, it slightly pre-dates my appointment. It is, unfortunately, symptomatic of the attitude of many British companies to exports.

I was asked by a Puerto Rican company if I could find out how they could import Pimm's. How they found out about Pimm's I have no idea. It is unknown in Puerto Rico although it is widely drunk in the Caribbean as well as, of course, in its home country, the U.K. I believe the formula is a secret but it is a refreshing summer drink that contains enough alcohol to catch up with you quite quickly.

I made appropriate inquiries in London and found that one of the oldest exporting houses dealing with the Caribbean had the distribution rights. I contacted them and asked for literature and samples. They sent me five brochures—one page folded in half— and two samples (miniatures). They sent them regular mail, which came by sea and took almost six weeks to reach me. A week after that I received a telex—you can see how long ago it was—expressing their disappointment that I had not yet closed an order for the first trailer load. I couldn't believe my ears, or eyes actually.

When I had calmed down from this piece of arrogant stupidity, I had to wonder if that was the way that British companies followed up sales leads. It was no wonder the empire went down the drain! Unfortunately my subsequent experience showed that, all too often, it was typical.

I contacted them again to explain that it was difficult to promote a major new product with five one-page brochures and a couple of miniatures. I was answered with a pompous diatribe that they had been trading in the Caribbean for over three hundred years and, basically, they knew what they were doing.

I was tempted to reply that, if they had been trading in the Caribbean for over three hundred years, I would take a pretty firm bet on what commodity they were trading when they started! I probably should have done it. I wasn't Honorary Consul then, so I didn't have to worry about being diplomatic, and they needed the wake-up call.

They remained adamant that they had sent me more than enough to produce a firm order, so I gave up and washed my hands of a losing proposition. It may not have produced a significant increase in Britain's exports but it all adds up, and such attitudes are just plain stupid and arrogant as well as being counter productive.

A great introduction to the world of developing British trade!

DEPORTATION IS FUN—PART TWO

"Even the U.S. Consular Service is not that dumb."

This case is not quite so stupid as the first one but anyone arrested for violating a deportation order doesn't deserve much sympathy.

I received a letter from a "Mrs. Jones"[1] requesting my help in the matter of her husband's arrest in San Juan. She said he was a British citizen and they resided in Trinidad.

The letter explained that the couple had lived as permanent

---

[1] Name has been changed.

residents in the United States for twenty-seven years before recently moving to Trinidad, her home, two years ago. A year after their arrival in Trinidad her husband returned to the U.S. to visit some family members. When he arrived at Miami Airport, he was detained by U.S. immigration officials. They allowed him into the U.S. but ordered him to report to their Baltimore office in three weeks time. His wife's letter said that he had planned to stay for longer than that so he duly reported on the designated day.

Why he didn't try to find out why he should report is beyond me.

In Baltimore, Immigration immediately arrested him and put him in jail for forty days while they reviewed his case. It turned out that he had been convicted in a drug-related incident ten years earlier. "But I served my time," he protested.

"Yes, you did," replied the immigration officials, "but the new immigration law requires all foreign citizens convicted of a felony, regardless of when they were convicted, to be deported to their home country."

They then proceeded to deport "Mr. Jones" to the U.K., his country of birth. So far, so good. You could forgive him for not knowing that immigration laws can be changed and can be applied retroactively. I'm amazed the U.S. got away with that, myself. However, now comes the really stupid part, although it is stupid of both him and the U.S. consular system. (I'm glad we're not the only ones!)

After deportation to the U.K. he immediately returned to his wife and family in Trinidad. He managed to get an engineering job with a large U.S. company that had operations in Trinidad. However, one of their requirements was that he go to the home office for training; the home office was in Ohio. He did have the presence of mind to go to the U.S. Embassy in Trinidad. According to his wife's letter they told him there was no record on their computers of any problem and they could certainly issue him a visa. This was April and he had been deported in January. Hello! The letter didn't say whether he told them about his deportation but I would assume not. Even the U.S. Consular Service is not that dumb.

He climbed on a plane, landed in Puerto Rico to connect with his flight to the mainland, and was promptly arrested for deportation violation. He was suddenly looking at three to four months before the case was heard and a possible jail term of five years.

I rest my case for stupidity.

CHAPTER XIV
SERIOUS

HURRICANE HUGO

"My image of him will always be swaggering down a street in St. Croix with a .45 on his hip and his boys following behind."

One of the downsides of living in the Caribbean is that, occasionally, the wind blows rather strongly and it rains quite heavily. Strongly and heavily enough, in fact, that it causes considerable damage at times. Hurricanes are not fun and should be avoided at all costs. I once had an offer to fly to London free on a British charter flight that was leaving just ahead of a hurricane—I should have taken it. I was called by the captain who had asked if they should stay and experience the hurricane. They were supposed to "dead-head" back through Miami a few days later. I strongly suggested that they "dead-head" back on the same plane on which they had arrived. It was then that they offered me a ride.

Hurricanes become very personal or, at least, the reactions to them become very personal. Although this story relates to the Honorary Consulate, personal memories are inevitably interwoven with the more official ones.

Hurricane Hugo was a powerful storm that did a great deal of damage in Puerto Rico and the Virgin Islands in 1992. It was the first hurricane to score a direct hit on Puerto Rico since I arrived on the Island more than fifteen years before, and from what I was told, for many years before that. The local population had lulled themselves into a false sense of security with wonderful stories about predicting the advent of hurricanes by watching how avocados ripened. Another favorite was that the island had become so industrialized that it produced enough extra heat to divert hurricanes away from its shores. As with most such tales there was a little bit of truth in each one but reliance on such predictions was somewhat flawed.

The Miami Hurricane Centre was the acknowledged expert in the field of predictions and, with a fleet of hurricane tracking planes, could provide badly needed warnings.

I often wonder what makes people take a job that involves deliberately and repeatedly flying through the eye of a hurricane. I'm glad they do it because it helps predict the landfalls of the storms, but it would not be my ideal as fun or a career path!

When Hurricane Hugo was approaching, the Miami Hurricane Centre predicted it would pass to the east of the U.S. Virgin Islands. The local weather forecaster in San Juan said they were wrong and that it would pass much further west—in other words straight for Puerto Rico.

People were a little concerned and started putting masking tape on their windows—a virtually useless precaution that looks good and convinces you that you are doing something useful. However, there was no real need to worry because the avocados had ripened quickly that year and hurricanes never hit Puerto Rico anyway.

Throughout the Caribbean there are well-known "hurricane holes." These are protected harbors that the test of time has shown are safe-havens for small boats. One such haven was in the main bay of Culebra; Culebra is one of Puerto Rico's two main off-shore islands, which together with the larger Vieques, are known as the Spanish Virgin Islands. As Hugo approached, many private and charter yachts from St. Thomas in the U.S. Virgin Islands and from Tortola in the British Virgin Islands, as well as many local Puerto Rican boats, headed for Culebra. An unofficial count placed well over two hundred yachts in the bay when the hurricane hit it full on.

Fifteen miles to the east in St. Thomas, U.S. Virgin Islands, the commander of the resident 110 ft. U.S. Coast Guard cutter was listening closely to the Miami Hurricane Centre. His command was a fast patrol boat that was usually in hot pursuit of drug traffickers in the area. He was torn between a gut reaction that told him to take his boat out to sea and out of the way of the storm and believing Miami that said the main force of the storm would pass to his east. His cutter had just undergone a several million dollar refit so he was particularly sensitive to potential damage. He decided to stay.

Back in Puerto Rico the hurricane was becoming much more of a reality. People were boarding up store windows and there was a run on all canned goods, bottled water, matches and anything else that looked as if it might be useful. I saw one person carrying a new deckchair out of the supermarket—they were going to sit on the beach and watch? I decided that living on the fifth floor of a condominium on the beach was not the right place to be, so I parked one car in my office underground parking and drove the family to a friend's concrete house a little further inland. We had moved all our furniture away from windows and, where possible, into corridors before leaving and hoping for the best. Not exactly a well-thought-out strategy but it was our first time.

We sat in the house with our friends and several others who had joined us and listened to the local English language radio station, which stayed on the air throughout the ordeal. The manager/broadcaster became quite a cult hero afterwards for remaining at his post despite walls falling in around him—literally. It's only at times like these you realize how important news really is.

The hurricane struck St. Croix in the U.S. Virgin Islands. It was a head-on attack. All communications immediately went out and stayed that way for many days. Not a good sign for those of us still waiting to be hit. The next to go was the British Virgin Islands. It disappeared under a communications blackout that also lasted for many days. The next in line was St. Thomas, then Culebra, and then the Puerto Rican mainland. The local forecaster had been right and Miami wrong, but that was not much consolation.

Suddenly the wind started picking up and the trees began to moan as they bent to unusual angles. Debris started flying by the windows of the house. We were all fascinated albeit a little scared. It is an interesting fact about hurricanes that most of the damage is caused by flying debris, not just by the wind itself, except in extreme cases—tin roofs are probably the worst missiles. We finally went to bed with the storm still causing havoc outside, but a general consensus among us that the house would survive. When we woke up, calm and the sun had returned but not, unfortunately, normality; no water, no electricity, but radio was still broadcasting and we had telephones, amazingly enough.

About mid-afternoon my host and I decided to brave the roads and see what had happened to my apartment. A journey that would normally take twenty minutes took almost an hour and a half. Debris covered the roads and it was like negotiating an obstacle course not to mention avoiding anything that looked like a wire—it might be live! I always regret not taking a video camera on that journey. Memory will have to serve.

The condominium looked like a disaster area. The roof had recently been sealed and the company had used concrete blocks to help secure the roofing membrane. Somehow the wind had managed to get under the membrane and the resulting motion had sent the blocks raining down on the parking lot below. I won't describe the cars that had been left there but the whole area was inches deep in shattered blocks. My apartment, fortunately, had suffered only minor damage caused when debris had shattered the front picture window. We had been extremely lucky.

Several weeks later I was privy to the Puerto Rican Air National Guard weather-tracking maps and the reason for San Juan's escape from the worst of the storm became quite clear. The eye of the hurricane was headed for San Juan after it hit Culebra, but the outer circulation of the storm hit the 3,000 ft. mountain that guards Puerto Rico's north-eastern region. The storm appeared to ricochet off the mountain and head due north for about twenty minutes before resuming its more westerly direction. That jog saved San Juan although it devastated the rain forest on the slopes of the mountain. The Virgin Islands did not fare quite so well.

One story that emerged from St. Thomas is tragic but funny at the same time. It was not public knowledge but I was told about it by an official who participated in the sequence of events. It concerned that Coast Guard's decision to keep their cutter in St. Thomas harbor or, rather, the commanding officer's decision to keep *his* cutter in St. Thomas harbor.

The Coast Guard command bunker in San Juan was monitoring all radio traffic and keeping track of its assets, and it was in touch with the cutter and its crew. The Captain reported that he realized the Miami Hurricane Centre's predictions were wrong and that the hurricane was about to hit St. Thomas with its full force. It was too late to move the cutter out so he and his crew would ride out the storm on board in the harbor. The staff in the command bunker feared the worst.

A little later the captain reported that he had issued the order to abandon ship and proceeded to shut down the radio link to his command. The bunker's listeners were convinced he had signed his crews' death warrants, albeit with an understandable order. The crew went to their assigned positions and abandoned ship… by walking down the gangplank onto the main harbor road. The storm surge had lifted the 110ft. cutter and deposited it in the centre of town. I don't know what happened to the captain's career but I could take a shrewd guess. A multi-million dollar refit with more than a few dents does not look good on a resume and someone had to take the blame.

A few weeks after the hurricane passed I was asked to go over to Culebra to help some British subjects who had lost everything on their yachts moored in the "hurricane hole." I could not believe the scene that greeted my arrival. Of the over two hundred yachts that had taken refuge there only ten were still floating. There were great piles of expensive fiberglass on the town quay. There were yachts sitting in mangrove swamps thirty and forty feet above the water line and many masts just sticking out of the water. There were tales of people who had decided to stay on their yachts. One, who had decided in the middle of the storm that it was too dangerous, had swum ashore. *Swum ashore in a hurricane!* Miraculously, no one appeared to have drowned. One of the people I had come to see owned one of the boats that were sitting up in the mangroves. His yacht had been a participant in the Whitbread "Round the World" race and so was built to withstand the worst of elements. He told me that his wind speed instruments had come off the mast at 240 knots. I'm glad I wasn't there and that we had El Yunque mountain in Puerto Rico to protect us.

Later that day I went back into Dewey, the main town, and the scene and atmosphere of total destruction was alleviated slightly when I went into one of the downtown drinking holes. (I needed to steady my nerves or, at least, that was the excuse.) A sign behind the bar read: "All unaccompanied children will be sold."

Someone had told me years before that the only difference between the sailors and wharf rats of the Caribbean today and those of a hundred years ago was that the eye patches have been removed. Selling children reinforced that story.

Finally, a story about St. Croix, which was probably hit the hardest by Hurricane Hugo. The devastation was so extreme that all civil control broke down. Solid concrete houses that cost millions had simply disappeared leaving only foundations. Infrastructure was virtually non-existent and there were stories, not for public consumption, of police seen looting while still dressed in their uniforms. I should add that this is not a banana republic we are talking about but a U.S. territory.

I had become close friends several years before with the "Agent in Charge" of the FBI's regional office in San Juan. St. Croix fell under his jurisdiction. He told me afterwards that they had to literally invade St. Croix and physically restore order. They went in on U.S. Navy and Coast Guard vessels fully armed. He joked once that he went to a town meeting and that all the people were quite respectful despite the fact that they resented the FBI presence. He said it may have had something to do with the fact that he went into the meeting with a .45 on his hip and a squad of agents carrying M16s behind him. He was the "warlord" of St. Croix for several weeks until Washington sent in National Guard units to supervise the restoration of some form of normality. My image of him will always be him swaggering down a street in St. Croix with a .45 on his hip and his boys following behind. Maybe the FBI should use that on a recruitment poster?

Anyone who thinks hurricanes are interesting, or even romantic and should be experienced first hand, should be left in no doubt. They aren't and they shouldn't be.

CHAPTER XV
POLITICALLY
INCORRECT CHUCKLES

These stories all appealed to my irreverent sense of humor. Such humor is frowned upon in some quarters and, if expressed in public, is likely to become tomorrow's headlines. However, it doesn't stop you chuckling when no one is looking or when you are amongst friends!

"West Indian Diplomacy" has to be one of my favorite stories. The situation had to be treated with appropriate decorum and outrage but once you let your imagination and sense of humor loose it was more likely to produce a script for a Hollywood comedy.

"Terrorizing Old Ladies" provided some exceptional entertainment once the real story became clear. However, it took a long time before anyone knew what on earth was going on!

"Episcopi Vagantes" is serious stuff. Renegade priests and bishops infesting the Caribbean sounds like a plot from a horror movie rather than a real dilemma. However, there's always a tendency to chuckle when the sanctity of the church is violated providing it's not too detrimental. Sort of makes it more human somehow!

Finally, "Claiming the Fortress" was a case where the authorities in charge really set themselves up for a fall. I enjoyed taking advantage but I think the fortress had the last laugh.

"…he was going to call himself 'The Queen of [insert name of island.'"

"Michael Caine move over" or, better still, "Michael, sorry, *Sir* Michael, here is the sequel to your film *Water*."

British territories in the Caribbean still fall under the jurisdiction of the British Colonial Office in London—at least they did when this story took place. I remember once having a discussion about this "politically challenged" office title with the Governor of one of these islands. He told me that he had started his career working as a district officer in Kenya under the Colonial Service just after World War II. He was finishing his career under the same Colonial Office, but as Governor of a British Territory in the Caribbean. I must admit that I would have thought that political correctness would have caught up with the British government long before the mid-1990s, but obviously not.

Governors of territories in the Caribbean still wear three-cornered hats with feathers on formal occasions (and you thought *Water* wasn't true to local life). Local customs require a great deal of formality and, since the communities are so small, appearances and decorum are extremely important.

Much to the amazement of many new governors, some people will not sit down until the governor sits and are reluctant to speak until they are spoken to—the governor is representing Her Majesty the Queen after all (no, this is not 1890—it *is* 1990).

One unmarried governor found, on arrival at his new post, that his secretary, who had worked in that post for many years, immediately resigned because "what would people say if she worked in an office with a man who was single!"

You begin to get the idea and thus will appreciate the heinous nature of what I am about to relate.

A new governor arrived on a small Caribbean island that was, and still is, a British territory. This man had a vast amount of experience in the British Foreign Service, was married, kept himself in good shape, and was generally liked by all who knew him. Aside from a delicious sense of humor—he once told me that, since he represented Her Majesty The Queen, he was going to call himself "The Queen of [insert name of island]." I don't think he did but I wouldn't have put it past him.

(I certainly warned him not to try it in San Juan unless he wanted to be rather more popular than I thought he would have appreciated!)

He was also a bicycle fanatic. He loved riding and, if possible, racing, bicycles. He even occasionally brought his bike to Puerto Rico to practice the velodrome that was built for the Pan American Games. Every Sunday morning, official duties permitting, he donned his cycling gear—shorts and a tee-shirt—and set off. Now the island concerned is quite small, and it doesn't take long to cover virtually all the roads that exist, so to get a decent workout he did several laps.

The local population took rather a dim view of their Queen's representative appearing publicly in shorts and riding a bicycle—surely a top hat and an old Rolls Royce, or even an old Daimler as in Michael Caine's case, would have been more appropriate. And on a Sunday as well! He should have been in the front row of the local church leading the congregation, as befitted someone of his rank! I don't know whether a complaint was actually filed against him but it is quite possible.

On Palm Sunday 1991 he was pedaling away, when he came to the only long downhill section on his course. The corner at the bottom was not too sharp and, if he lined it up correctly, he didn't have to brake to get around. He came barreling down the hill, swung round the corner, only to be faced with a flock of elderly ladies coming out of church all dressed in their finest Sunday clothes. There was nowhere to go. He went straight through the middle, knocking over several matriarchs, and crashed in a heap of dust on the side of the road. Oh for a video camera! Fortunately no one was seriously hurt, at least not physically, but the Governor's reputation came to rest somewhere in the deep ocean trench that borders the island.

The vicar came running out of the church and demanded to know what had happened and who was responsible. When he realized the Governor was to blame, his indignation got the better of his respect for that high office. "How could you behave so irresponsibly, on a Sunday, and on Palm Sunday at that?" he screamed. The Governor drew himself up to his full height and replied with attempted decorum, which was a little difficult considering his appearance, "I don't care, I'm an atheist."

That made the front page of *The Times* and certainly contributed to his early retirement from government service.

Don't you think that would make a great basis for a sequel to the film *Water*? The image of the crash makes me chuckle every time I think about it and the incident probably heads the list in the annals of the politically incorrect.

TERRORIZING OLD LADIES

"…they…tried to entice two septuagenarians to dance with them."

We have all witnessed the strange antics of tourists at one time or another. Being a tourist appears to endow people with the right to behave in ways that they would not dream of exhibiting at home. Of course this has never been the case with you or I but it certainly seems to be common among those other tourists!

Puerto Rico is a Caribbean island and, although tourism represents less than ten per cent of its economy—manufacturing is forty per cent and the balance is service industries and government—it does receive its fair share of tourist problems.

I received a call one day from a member of the general public—his definition not mine—stating that some members of the

British Army had landed on one of San Juan's beaches. Just what I needed to hear on a Monday morning!

I was not aware that we had invaded Puerto Rico again. The last time we tried was in 1797 and maybe we were coming back to avenge that defeat. Since an honorary consul would be the last to be informed and, even then, certainly not by his own government, it was always a possibility, however remote. After all, one of the Island's economic czars asked me several times for a British passport based on the fact that the island had been a British colony for three months in the 1600s. So maybe a deal had been struck. Who was I to know?

I told the caller that I would talk to the local police and get to bottom of this seemingly unlikely event. However, before I could do that I received another call. This time from the owner of a small hotel close to the beach. He reported that several British Army personnel had ransacked his lobby and terrorized his guests. Invasion was sounding more likely by the minute! I looked out of my office window to see if I could see a landing craft or warships offshore—I am lucky enough to be able to see that part of the Atlantic Ocean from my eleventh floor office window. Nothing!

Perhaps I should add a little background here. Puerto Rico is United States territory. There are significant U.S. Navy and Army installations on the island and, in fact, the large navy base of Roosevelt Roads, as you may remember from a previous story, was originally built to house the British Home Fleet if Hitler had invaded the U.K. in World War II. However, there are no British units stationed there and thus the whole story seemed a little far-fetched. Still, there had been two independent reports.

The Puerto Rican State Department then called to ask what I knew about the incidents. Obviously the police had reported it to them and they had called me. This was getting serious but I had no information. I said I would try and find out and call them back.

At this point the first caller called back to say that the soldiers were now terrorizing old ladies on the beach. I decided I had to go and see for myself. Driving over there I realized I was hardly dressed for expeditions to the beach. If I had taken a bowler hat and an umbrella I would have matched the consular profile perfectly. However, when I got there the "soldiers" had vanished and I could not see any tank tracks on the sand. Wonderful! I wondered what to do.

I called the British Embassy in Washington DC, the home of my senior diplomatic boss and of the British Defense Attachés for the United States. They could provide no information but suggested I talk with the commanders of the local U.S. bases and then call them back. I should have known better than ask questions—it just ended up making me more responsible to more people.

I spoke to the commanders of the navy base and the army base and neither of them knew anything about marauding British troops. Where the hell had they come from? Perhaps they landed from a submarine. Unlikely, someone would have seen it. If it had been one report I might have thought the observers were mistaken, but three independent reports seemed to be overwhelming evidence.

I then thought of the Royal Navy's Flag Officer for the Caribbean, who was based in Barbados. I called him and he didn't know either. This was becoming intriguing as well as frustrating. I know the British Special Air Service (SAS) are good at blending in to any community but what on earth would they be doing in Puerto Rico when the U.S. Military appeared to have no knowledge of their presence? Perhaps this was a preliminary strike in the recapture of our errant colony, the U.S.?

The investigation eventually led to the Puerto Rican National Guard. They have a firing range on the south coast of the island, which is part of a larger training base. "Yes," they said, "a squad of Royal Marines was there on exercises." Apparently the British Army had a training agreement with the U.S. National Guard system, of which the Puerto Rican National Guard is part, and a squad of "British soldiers" was exercising under air cover on that base. At least I had found them. Now what on earth were they doing practicing on public beaches in San Juan?

It turned out that some fool of a British officer had authorized a weekend off in San Juan on the beach for these lads without supervision. After training hard for several weeks they were simply let loose. They arrived in San Juan, found the closest bar to the beach and proceeded to become paralytically drunk. They had done some minor damage in the hotel, mainly by falling over furniture, but on the beach they had started singing and dancing.

Realizing they only had each other to dance with they had, apparently, tried to entice two septuagenarians to dance with them. Hence the report of terrorizing old ladies. They disappeared, presumably back to their training on the south coast.

It seemed rather pointless following this up since the soldiers were due to deport Puerto Rico in a couple of days. However, I was tempted to track down the two septuagenarians to see if they enjoyed their dance! I would rather believe that it was the reporter who thought they were being terrorized rather than the ladies themselves! The image still makes me chuckle.

EPISCOPI VAGANTES

"…the idea of a renegade priest does have a tendency to make you chuckle…"

Some things ought to be sacrosanct but, in this case, they most certainly are not. Renegade priests, impostors posing as priests and even priests posing as members of churches to which they don't belong, all seem somewhat unlikely scenarios. However, in the Caribbean they appear to be flourishing. A letter from the office of the Archbishop of Canterbury in England confirmed the fact.

That letter also requested that I inform the local authorities that there were people in the Caribbean posing as bishops of the Anglican Church, no less. I suppose a mere priest would not have enough drawing power for fund-raising, which was apparently what they were doing. The letter contained a list of all the official Anglican Bishops in the region in case anyone had any doubts.

It is rather a delicate situation when you have to inform the local authorities that persons unknown are impersonating church officials from an institution that is the religious backbone of your country.

However, I duly informed them and sent a copy of my letter to the only "real" bishop resident in Puerto Rico. He called me and we discussed the problem. He indicated that it was significant enough to have occupied discussion time at a recent Anglican convention in Panama and that it would also be the subject of further discussion at a conference in London later that year. (How many renegades priests are there running around? Maybe I should ask for formal identification in future before listening to sermons and certainly before donating any money to their causes!)

The local bishop wrote back to the Archbishop of Canterbury and sent me a copy. His reply included the names of two known impostors in Puerto Rico together with the addresses of their churches. It is tempting to wonder, if they knew who these impostors were and where they preached, why they didn't denounce them!

I have not heard anything further on this topic and, to the best of my knowledge, I have never endorsed a false priest. Come to think of it I have never endorsed a bona fide one either! However, the idea of a renegade priest does have a tendency to make you chuckle even if that reaction is somewhat sacrilegious.

Some things should be sacrosanct!

RECLAIMING THE FORTRESS

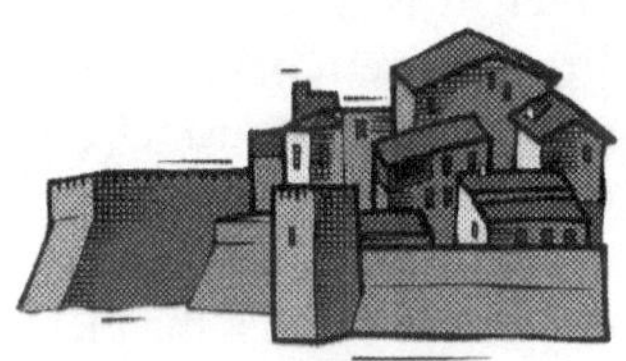

"Part way through my speech the fates took a hand. A strong gust of wind blew over the flag, to a great burst of laughter from the audience."

In 1797 Sir Ralph Abercromby attacked San Juan, Puerto Rico with the intention of securing the island for British interests and preparing the new colony for the arrival of a group of planters and their families. He had left England in 1796 with a charge from the Secretary of State, Henry Dundas, to secure the colony of St. Domingue (present-day Haiti) and to capture Puerto Rico and Trinidad. He was also ordered to relocate as many St. Domingue planters and their families as possible. How he was to do this, and in what order, was left up to him. Just before he sailed a letter arrived from London telling him to ignore St. Domingue and concentrate on Trinidad and Puerto Rico.

Such broad, imprecise, and often conflicting instructions were common in those days because the Ministers back in London often had little practical knowledge of the Caribbean. What intelligence they did possess was usually vague and years old—not their personal intelligence I hasten to add, although that is debatable given some of the ministers who were involved.

Abercromby decided to start with an attack on Trinidad.

He sailed into the Gulf of Paria Soon on February 17, 1797. A Spanish squadron was anchored in Chagaramus Bay so he sent his boats in to observe the enemy fleet. However, as soon as Abercromby's boats approached the Spanish sailors set fire to their own ships and rowed ashore.

In quick order the garrison on the shore installations surrendered, the Governor of the island's main town, Port of Spain, capitulated, and Abercromby found himself the conqueror of Trinidad without having to fire a shot.

Caribbean islands were often used as bargaining chips by the countries of France, Spain, the Netherlands, and England in their wars against each other. It is true that certain private Caribbean landowners pushed their governments to protect commerce, but much of the apparent game of "musical islands" was related to European politics and wars and not to the inherent value of the islands themselves. The other interesting fact about the fall of Trinidad to the English fleet was the manner in which they dealt with the Spanish incumbents. Warfare was much more brutal in those days but it was also much more gentlemanly. The Spanish officers were allowed to keep their personal effects and their swords and any landowner retained full rights to his property. Spanish Administration officials could even remain on the island

and retain their property if they swore allegiance to the British crown. Amazing!

Abercromby secured the colony of Trinidad and pressed on to his next objective. He stopped in Martinique to await reinforcements from England and, in April 1797, set sail for the Spanish-held island of Puerto Rico.

He passed St. Kitts on April 15 and briefly dropped anchor near Tortola, British Virgin Islands on April 16 to allow some of his squadron to catch up.

The British fleet was observed approaching Puerto Rico's north coast on Monday April 17. Naval intelligence in those days was at least as big an oxymoron as it is today and so Abercromby had little idea of the defensive forces ranged against him. He soon found out.

The fortresses of the capital city, San Juan, which were called El Morro and San Cristobal, had been designed by Irish engineers and were formidable and well-manned. Abercromby landed his troops to the east of San Juan and laid siege to the city. However, he quickly realized that he stood no chance of defeating the garrison with the resources at his disposal and so, on May 2, he left for greener pastures or, at least, less well-fortified locations.

Puerto Rico has always celebrated this event as the defeat of the British fleet. They may be stretching the truth a little but, if Abercromby had succeeded, the subsequent history of the island could have been very different.

In 1997, two Puerto Rican historians published a book on the events surrounding the attack by Abercromby. It was the first time, to anyone's knowledge, that extensive research in the U.K., as well as in Puerto Rico and Spain, had been devoted to the topic. The occasion of the book's publication was marked by a formal ceremony held in the San Cristobal fortress which had successfully guarded the city against the British attack.

Several weeks before the ceremony I received a call from one of the authors. She had been a colleague of mine when I was teaching at the local university many years before. She invited me to attend the ceremony. I said I wasn't sure I wanted to attend a ceremony that commemorated the defeat of the British. London might take a dim view of their representative on the island supporting a British defeat, even though it was two hundred years ago. She then upped the ante by asking me to speak at the event and promised I could say anything I wished. I immediately succumbed to such bribery and let my mind run riot with possible wordings. (The thought of a possible lynching did, however, rein in my imagination. Still, the opportunity was intriguing.)

A week before the event she called again and asked me if I could bring a British flag. I have to admit I was slightly incredulous. "You really want a British flag flying over San Cristobal at such a ceremony?" I asked. I was assured it was no problem and would, in fact, be welcome. The lynching looked a little closer!

The day dawned and I duly arrived at the San Cristobal fortress replete with my flag and flagpole (I did refrain from wearing a "redcoat" uniform, however). I asked where I should put the flag and was told to place it behind the podium in, what to me, was the position of precedence. Who was I to argue?

The time approached for the ceremony to start and no other flags had appeared. The Puerto Rican Department of State was well represented as were many private organizations and prominent people. No one seemed to notice that there was only one flag flying and I was not about to let such an opportunity pass by reminding them. When it came time for my speech I couldn't resist. I said, "I was slightly apprehensive about officially attending a ceremony to celebrate the defeat of my country. However, I feel that my attendance is vindicated, and I must say I am more than gratified, by seeing that the appropriate flag now flies over San Cristobal for the first time in two hundred years." Fortunately they laughed. There were, after all, many dungeons right below me!

A little later in my speech the fates took a hand. A strong gust of wind blew over the flag, to a great burst of laughter from the audience.

I'm sure the fortress smiled!

CHAPTER XVI
WHY THESE
STORIES?

The fundamental reason for including stories in this book, and excluding the many others, is that these are the ones I remember. That may sound a little redundant, since it would have been quite difficult to include those I didn't remember, but let me explain.

Over a period of fifteen years there were a large number of incidents that could have qualified under the chapter headings of this book. However, choices had to be made otherwise the book would have been endless and impossible to read. I therefore chose to include those that immediately sprang to mind. To exclude those I couldn't remember was obviously quite easy!

Many of the stories deserve a more comprehensive coverage—"The Birth Mother" and "Cuban Refugees" come to mind. However, in the context of this book, an extended narrative on any one story would have destroyed the balance I have tried to maintain.

I really can't tell you why these particular stories sprang to mind. They must all have that special something that still registered in my rapidly diminishing mental capacity. Perhaps it is the irreverent humor content or perhaps it is the emotional content that touched my sensitivities and thus prodded my memory. Whatever the case, I trust you have enjoyed them.

I had not planned to write a concluding chapter. It seemed redundant and anti-climatic. However, during the editing phase, it occurred to me that a sense of closure and a sense of continuance were both appropriate.

Many of these stories would form excellent bases for future novels—a challenge I may well pursue. Equally, there must be thousands of such stories out there and I would be delighted to hear from other honorary consuls about their experiences.

www.ingramcontent.com/pod-product-compliance
Lightning Source LLC
Chambersburg PA
CBHW051454250726
48655CB00001B/413